HOW TO DRAW POND LIFE

## ACKNOWLEDGMENT

In writing this book, I am indebted to John Clegg's *Fresh-water Life of the British Isles* (Frederick Warne & Co) for general information about water, water-weeds and snails, and to Malcolm Smith's *The British Amphibians & Reptiles* (Collins' *New Naturalist* series) for information about the breathing of frogs. Facts about primitive fish and Jurassic fossils have been verified from *Britain's Structure & Scenery* by L. Dudley Stamp (Collins' *New Naturalist* series). My thanks are due to the respective publishers for permission to use this information.

# HOW TO DRAW
# POND LIFE

by

# VERE TEMPLE

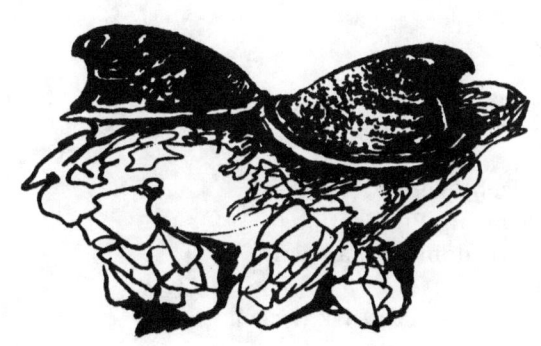

*

To my brother Peter

*

*How to Draw Pond Life*, by Vere Temple
Copyright © 2013 Coachwhip Publications
No claims made on public domain material.
First published 1956.
Front cover: Crested newt larva © Dirk Ercken

ISBN 1-61646-192-6
ISBN-13 978-1-61646-192-8

CoachwhipBooks.com

# Contents

# *Introduction*

WHEN EXPLORING THE COUNTRYSIDE I am always on the look-out for ponds; for a pond is a country, with geography and inhabitants. Under its waters, and on its shores, lives an animal and insect people which, like a human population, is for ever coming and going. New inhabitants arrive, either for a visit, or for the span of their lives; others depart. And as a country holds people of different tribes and races, so the pond's people belong to various orders: fishes, frogs, newts, dragonflies, beetles, snails and many others.

Just as a human population is composed of old and young—men and women, children and babies—so the pond's people live side by side, old and young alike, but with this difference: a human being is born into the world more or less in the shape it will retain throughout life, whereas frog and newt and dragonfly and beetle pass through different stages, and appear in different forms before reaching their mature or perfect form. And very extraordinary their shapes are, as we shall see. These pond babies are so unlike their parents that they appear as changelings, creatures from a goblin world. They grow quickly and their appearance changes as they grow, and if you miss one stage you must wait a whole year before their own children in their turn have reached the same stage. So why not make drawings of these pond children in their different stages? On an opposite page you may paste a drawing of the same creature in the mature state. You will then have a record of the whole life-cycle and some pages to show to your friends.

Pond creatures are splendid subjects for pencil or crayon drawings and for brush-work too. Their shapes are hard and definite and their bodies are beautifully constructed and there is no fur or fluff to confuse you. They are small in size and there is room for several drawings on one page. You will need a magnifying glass or a small hand lens to show you the details, and the articulation of the joints.

With a pond net you may dredge the creatures from the water and from the mud and leaves at the bottom of the pond. Jam-jars with loop-handles of string are useful containers for fish and tadpoles, while dragonfly nymphs (as the early stages are called) travel quite well in wet pond-weed, packed in tins. If you haven't an aquarium, old wash-basins floored with mud and gravel, placed out-of-doors, are roomy homes for the creatures you wish to keep under observation.

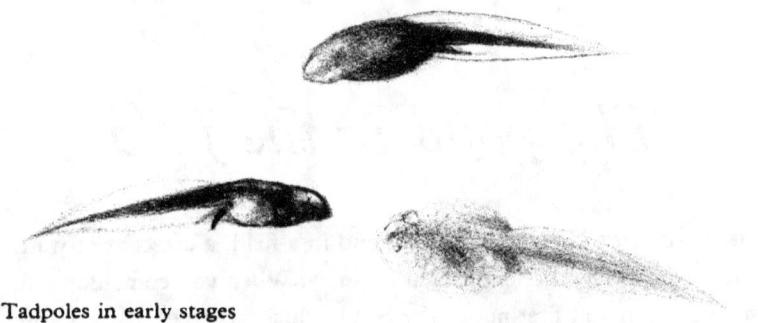

Tadpoles in early stages

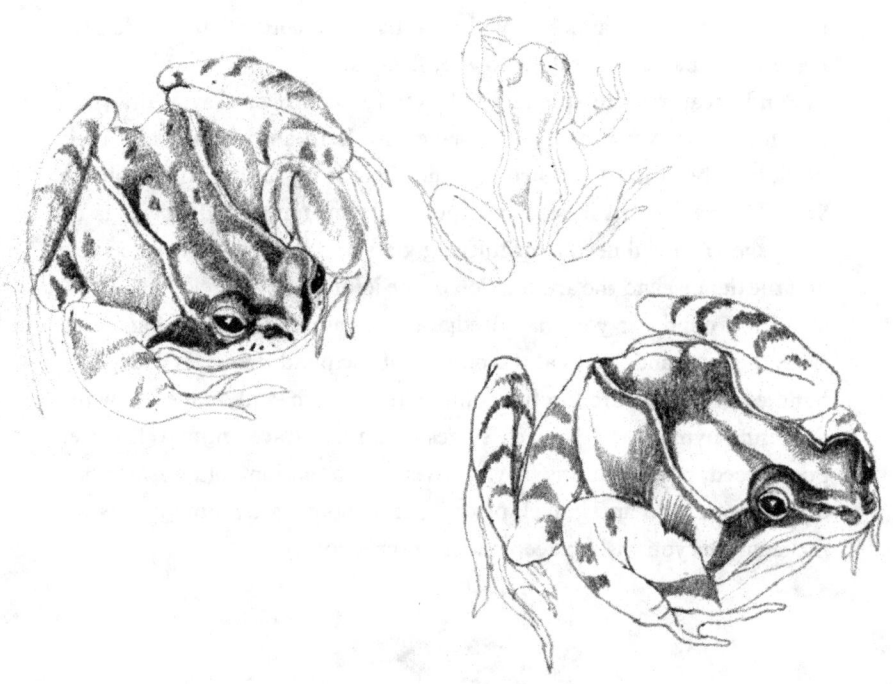

# *The pond in the field*

THE POND THAT I KNOW BEST is a pond in a field; a crescent of water, lying in the dip of the long, tilted meadow. When you come down the lane, you do not at first notice the pond, which is screened by a grove

The Frog is a bony creature: observe the curve of its skull,
the line of its spine, and the angular joints of its long hind legs

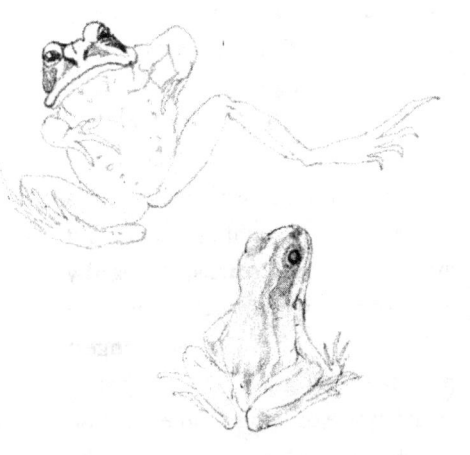

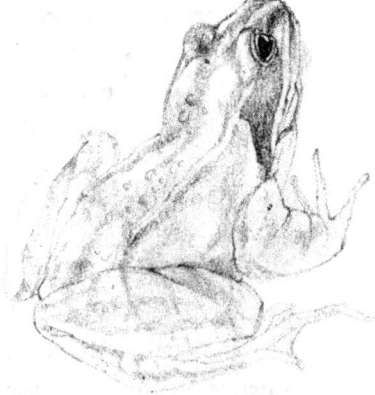

Its squatting attitude is like yours
when you hammer nails.

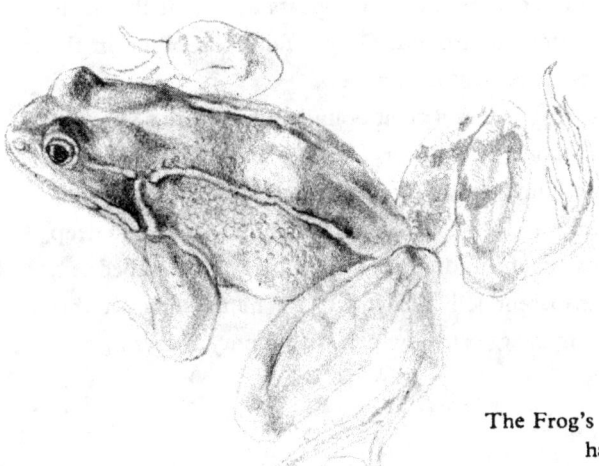

The Frog's little hands, flattened to earth,
have three fingers and a thumb.
Its dumpy forearms are rigid and the
webbed hind feet turn out more than yours.

of ancient laurel trees. Then, through the boles, you see the glint of water. You scramble over the fence and down through the trees, and there, below you, is the pond, open to the sun on the south. The water lends a stillness to the landscape, gathering to itself the shifting shadows and light. As an eye gives life to a face, so the pond gives life to the field. It holds the earth; it holds the sky; it is at once the mirror and the reality.

In winter, the pond was covered by a film of ice that shut off the water from the freezing air above. Beneath this protecting sheet, the pond creatures survived. Ice and snow melted under February rains, and now the March sun is warm. The air is full of new smells; the earthy smell of damp leaf-mould, the fragrance of violets and the heady smell of rising sap and growing things, which comes in whiffs and is strongest when you lie on your face among the soft young grasses by the pond-side. Nose to earth, you suddenly become aware of two round eyes close to yours. You had not noticed the frog (*Rana Temporaria*) to whom the eyes belonged, so rigidly crouched, that it appears as one of the many chunks of wood that litter the ground. Only a faint throbbing in the bag-like throat shows that the creature is alive.

Then, suddenly, the frog makes a great bound and is off in a series of leaps into the pond: *her* pond, her nursery, her home. She lays her eggs in shallow water on the sunny side of the pond, so that her children may benefit from the sunshine and be safe from the enemies that lurk in deep water. Her spawn consists of hundreds of round black eggs imbedded, for protection, in transparent jelly. If you bring home some of this spawn you must put it in a large shallow pan with plenty of fresh green

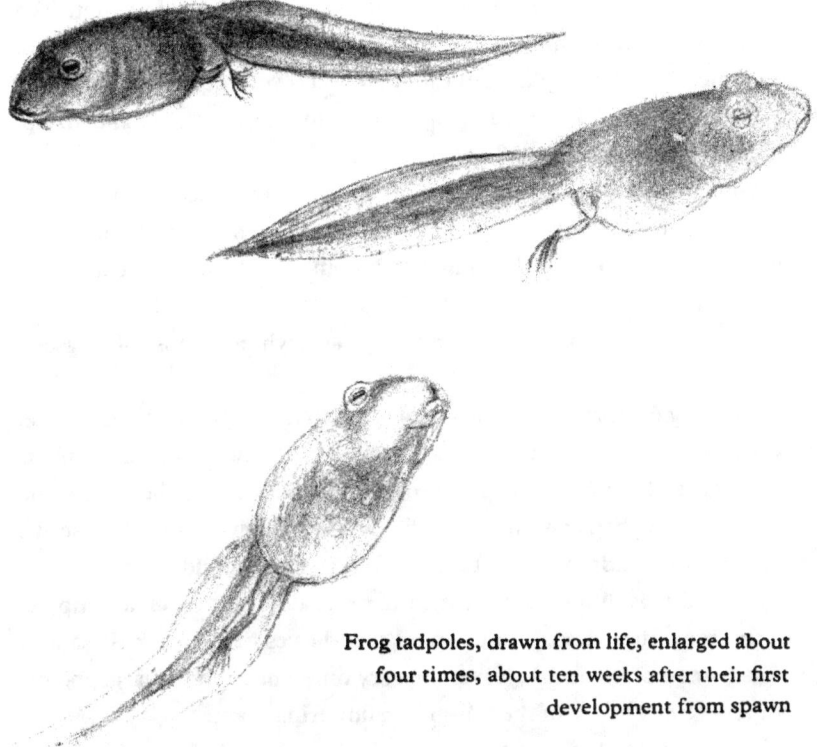

Frog tadpoles, drawn from life, enlarged about
four times, about ten weeks after their first
development from spawn

waterweed. This aerates the water and harbours tiny living creatures
upon which the tadpoles will feed when they begin to develop in about
two weeks' time. The round eggs elongate and grow tails and the small

tadpole frees itself from the now liquefied jelly and swims about. Ten weeks more and the hind legs are formed. Twelve weeks, counted from the time of the development of the spawn, and you see not a tadpole but a long-tailed frog. It can run along the bottom of the pond, and sit up, frogwise, with its long tail flowing behind it.

Young frogs often choose thunder-weather, with heavy rain, as the moment for leaving the water. Then, their tails shrink to a short stub which in its turn is absorbed into the system. The little frogs emerge on to dry land and disperse.

The tadpoles of toads (*Bufo bufo*) are black, whereas those of frogs are brown.

You may compare a tadpole's growth to that of a young plant or tree, which, whilst immature, continually sends forth new buds and shoots from its tender stem, until full growth is attained; and then grows no more, but toughens and hardens and produces flowers and then seeds. The plant's children grow from seeds; the frog's children grow from eggs. Seedlings differ from the mature plant almost as much as tadpoles differ from frogs. Look at the round seed-leaves of the pink Balsam or Touch-me-not; their first leaves are very different from the large, pointed, red-veined leaves of the full-grown flowering plant.

Plants breathe through their leaves in every stage of growth; but the breathing apparatus of the tadpole becomes completely changed in the frog. The tadpole breathes through gills, like those of a fish, placed behind the head; but the frog breathes through lungs placed inside its body just as are yours and mine, and those of cats and dogs, mice and birds.

These tadpoles at twelve weeks old, are almost Frogs
They can run about and sit frogwise. Pencil drawing.

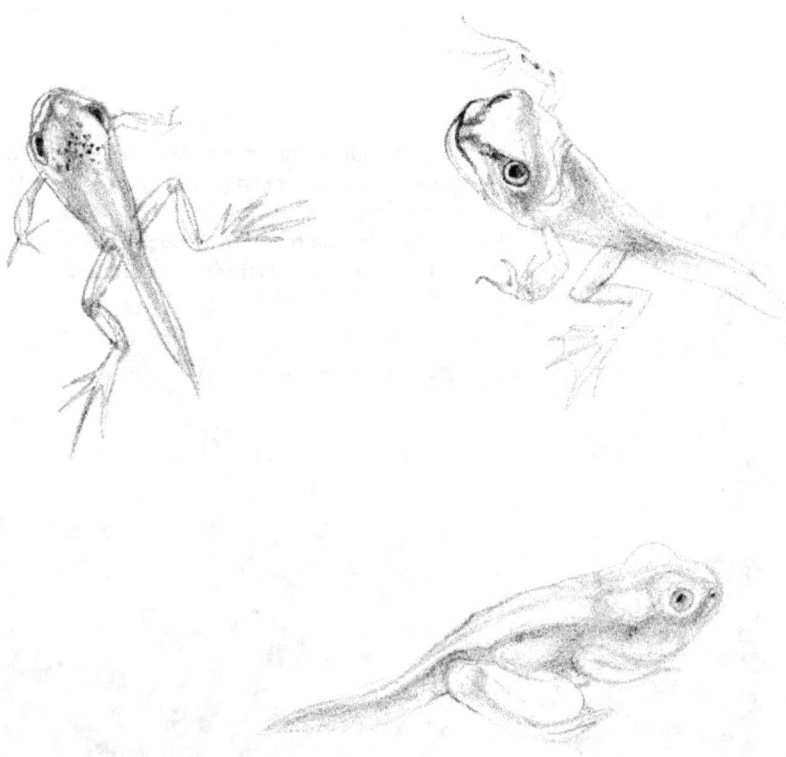

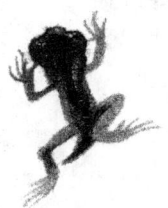
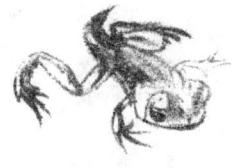

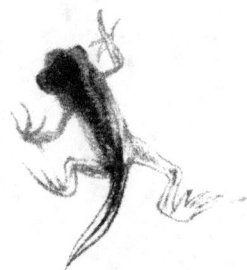

Water-colour drawings of Toad tadpoles ready
to leave the water and (below) young emerging
on to dry land.
As a tadpole it breathed through gills like those
of a fish; now it breathes through lungs.

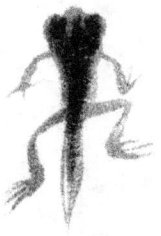
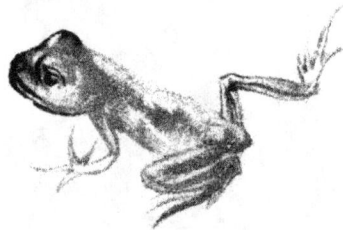

Chalk and pencil drawing of a male Great Crested Newt.
He is the largest of the three species of newts found in Great Britain

15

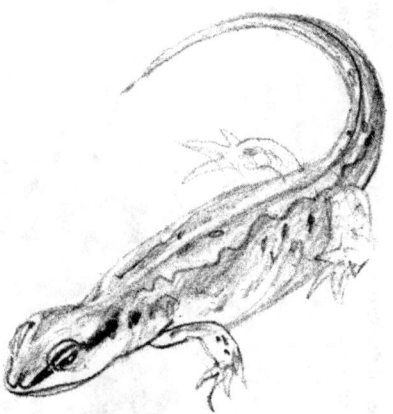

Pencil studies of the female Palmate Newt. The
mother newt lays her eggs singly and wraps them
up in the leaves of water plants. The tadpoles are
at first flat and transparent and could be mistaken
for small fishes.

But the frog differs from warm-blooded animals in that it has no ribs encasing its lungs. There is therefore no expansion of its body when it breathes; only the pulsation of the throat shows that air is being drawn through its nostrils into its lungs and out again. This way of breathing is characteristic of the adults of the class *Amphibia*, which comprises frogs, toads and newts. All these creatures are found in water in the spring and early summer breeding season only. At other times of year they lie up in sheltered places. Toads hibernate, often underground; frogs and newts tuck themselves into crannies at the mouth of a well or among damp leaves and ferns in the recesses outside windows that ventilate cellars.

Pencil study of a male Palmate Newt
which has webbed hind feet during the breeding season.

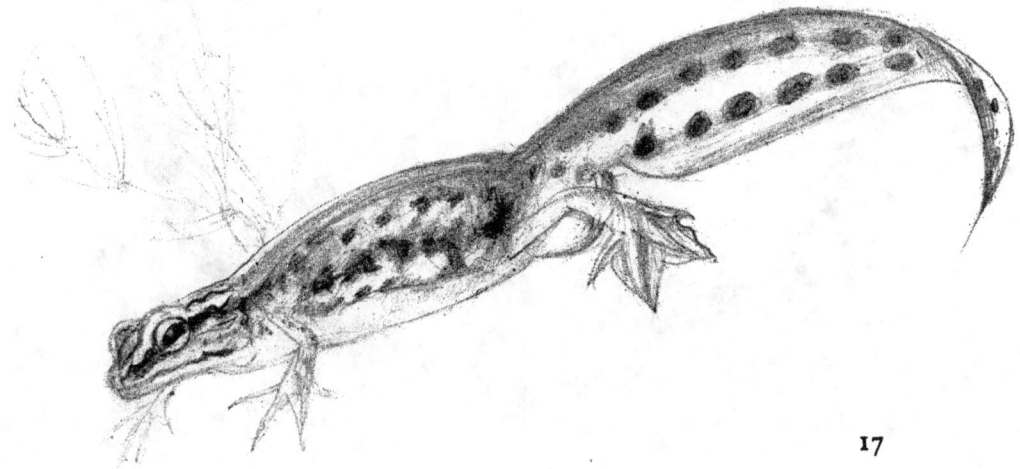

17

Newts are more graceful than frogs. With their long tails and mottled surface patterns they are indeed beautiful little creatures and repay time and trouble spent in studying them. We have three species: the Smooth Newt (*Triturus Vulgaris*), the larger and less common Warty or Great Crested Newt (*Triturus cristatus*) and the Palmate Newt (*Triturus helveticus*) which has webbed feet during the breeding season. The mother newt lays her eggs singly and wraps them up in the leaves of water plants. The resulting tadpoles are at first flat and transparent—you might mis-

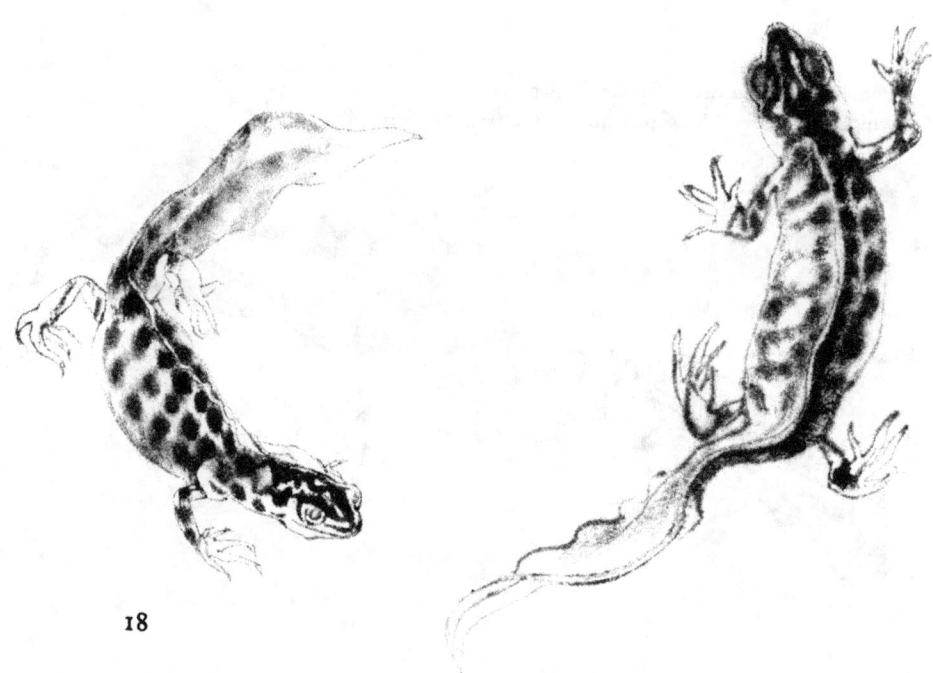

Water-colour drawings of male Smooth Newts.

They are, as you can see, far more graceful than frogs, and have a beautiful mottled surface pattern. One of them was about to hibernate and had partly lost its crest.

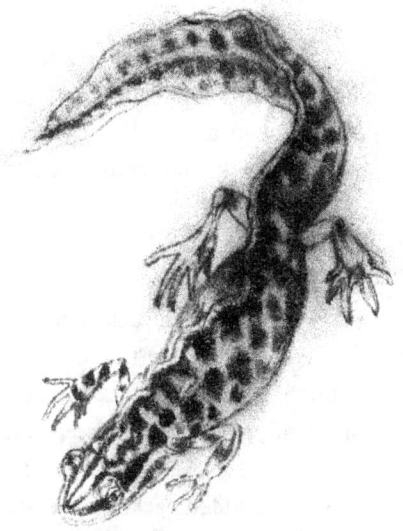

take them for small fishes. They soon grow legs, and their breathing gills behind the head assume a branched and feathery form.

Here are some pencil outline studies of newts, and some more complete drawings. An outline may be looked upon as a boundary, enclosing the form of the creature depicted. Boundaries on land, or in a garden, may sometimes be shifted; but you must never shift the boundary outline of a form when you record it on paper. If you do, the drawing will show a deformed version of the beautiful living creature.

19

Newts are long-lived creatures and do well in captivity; if you house them suitably you can watch their life-cycle, from year to year. Their requirements are space, cleanliness and adequate food. Earthworms and tadpoles are eaten greedily by the Great Crested Newt, small worms by the smaller species and all should be given bunches of fresh water-weed so that they can feed on the small creatures it harbours. A pile of stones should be arranged to form caves and grottoes below the surface of the water and above it a rocky eminence on which the newts can sit when the time comes for them to move to dry land. For a week, maybe, they will sit on their rocks, entwined to preserve moisture; then they may begin to climb the glass and to creep under the lid of the tank, which should fit tightly to prevent their escape. It is now time to move them into a ventilated, lidded packing case, standing on bricks in a shady spot out-of-doors. Six inches of earth, grass roots and caves made of half-bricks, will ensure them a snug hibernaculum. If the weather remains mild and damp during November and early December the newts will crawl about. Their appearance has altered considerably. Gone are the wavy crests: the bright colours and mottling have changed to black or rusty brown.

At the onset of cold weather, the Smooth and Palmate Newts creep into their caves. The Great Crested Newts crawl under the roots of grass. The hibernaculum should then be placed inside a larger box packed loosely with straw, and the containers moved under cover of some shed sheltered from raw frosts.

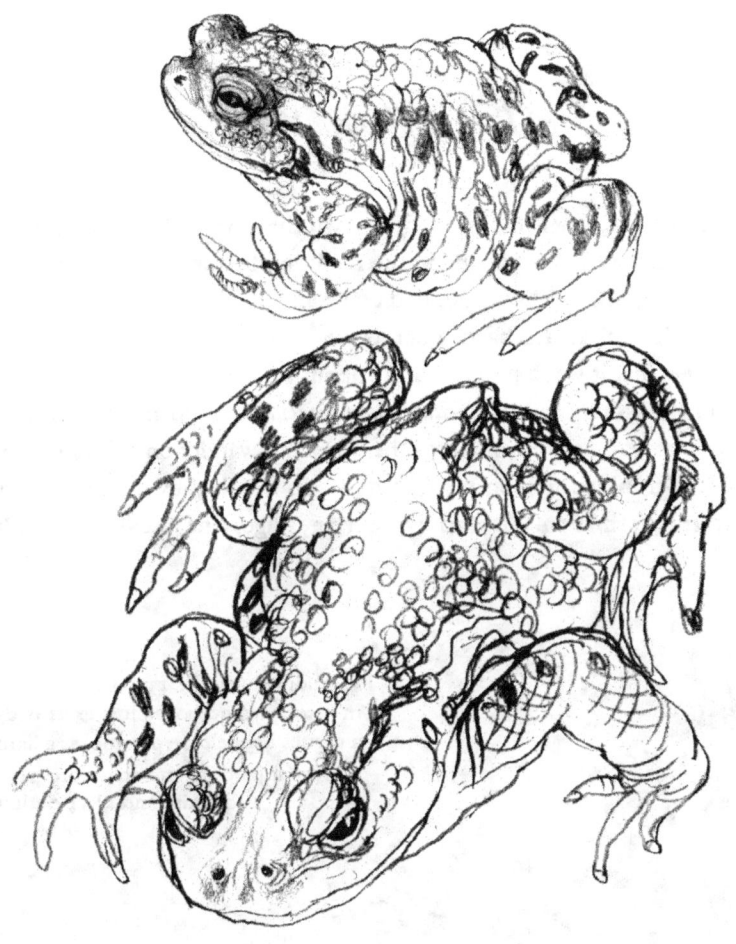

When digging potatoes in September I unearthed the Toad also.
He was carefully replaced in his hibernaculum.

# *Dragonflies*

ONE MAY DAY, when I was walking down the lane to the pond, I met a strange creature, also walking in the roadway. It was squat and clumsy, with six legs and a yellow-speckled belly; and it had a contraption rather like a child's bib folded back under its face.

I knew that it was a pond creature about to turn into its perfect form, that of a dragonfly called *Libellula quadrimaculata*. When these nymphs are full-grown, they crawl out of the pond and wander on till they come to a tree-trunk or sloping piece of bark, up which they climb to await their transformation. At this wandering stage, the creature already

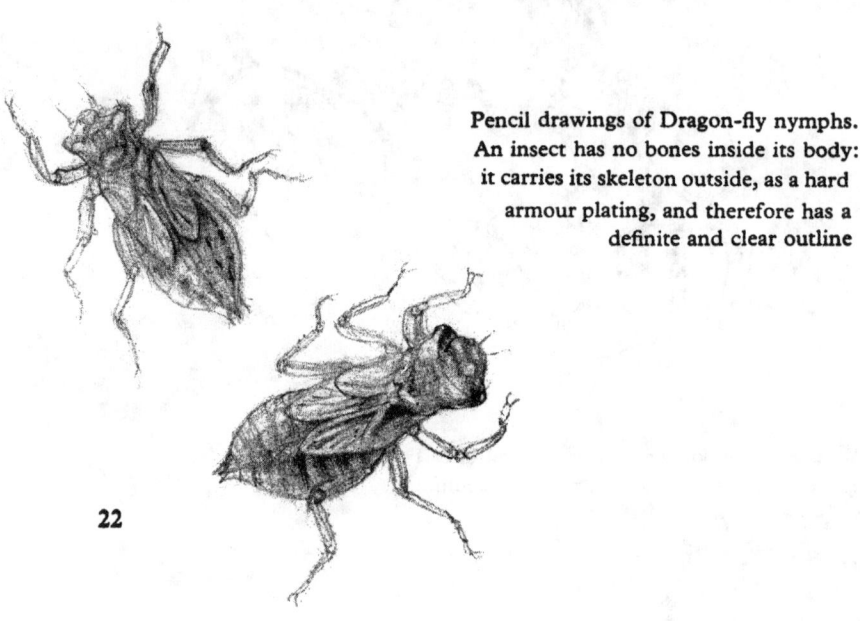

Pencil drawings of Dragon-fly nymphs. An insect has no bones inside its body: it carries its skeleton outside, as a hard armour plating, and therefore has a definite and clear outline

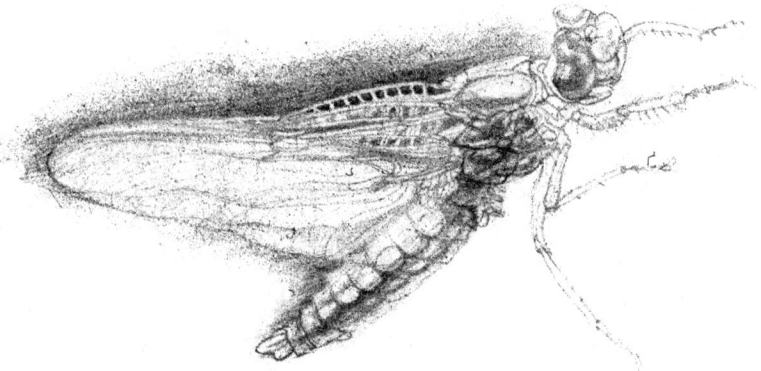

Dragon-fly, newly emerged from the empty shell of its nymph,
its long wings folded over its back

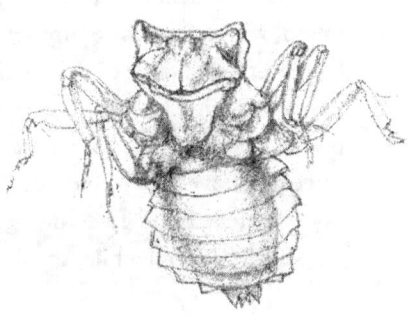

Full-grown Dragon-fly nymph,
a squat and clumsy creature with six legs
and a yellow-speckled belly,
with a contraption rather like a child's bib
folded back below its face

breathes air from the atmosphere, taken in through the spiracles or breathing holes at each side of its body. But when it lived in the pond it took in oxygen filtered from the water by an apparatus at its tail end.

Once at a reservoir, I saw scores of these dead nymphs floating upside-down on the water. The poor things, ready for their final transformation, had tried to climb up the steep concrete sides of the reservoir on which their claws could not get a grip. They were drowned because the water had got into their breathing holes, which at this stage of their existence are already open and ready to function (but it is easy for these slow, clumsy creatures to crawl out of the gently sloping rough banks of a pond).

Remembering this sad episode, I was particularly careful of my find on this May day. I took the creature home and housed it among moss and bits of sloping bark under a muslin net. That evening was one of suspense. The creature remained huddled in a corner. But next morning very early—so early that there was as yet no colour in the world out-of-doors—I unfastened the muslin tent and with my torch illumined the cage.

There, suspended, was the empty husk of the crawling thing I had found, with a few white threads hanging out of a hole in its back. Above the empty shell an exquisite being perched, its long wings folded over its back. White, like foam, with a foam-bubble's irridescence, the creature seemed hardly to live—but as I watched, I perceived that a greenish tinge crept over the round head and down the long jointed body. As the sky brightened, the green deepened, changing to golden yellow, slashed with black. After a while, the dragon fly scratched its head with its front

24

leg. With a jerk and a rustle, it spread out its four great wings, ready to swoop, to soar, to hover over the pond whence it came.

There are dragonfly nymphs of other kinds also to be found in the pond in the field—long ferocious brown ones and tiny slender green ones with leaf-like appendages at their tail ends. These smaller creatures

Dragon-fly (*Libellula quadrimaculata*) with wings outspread

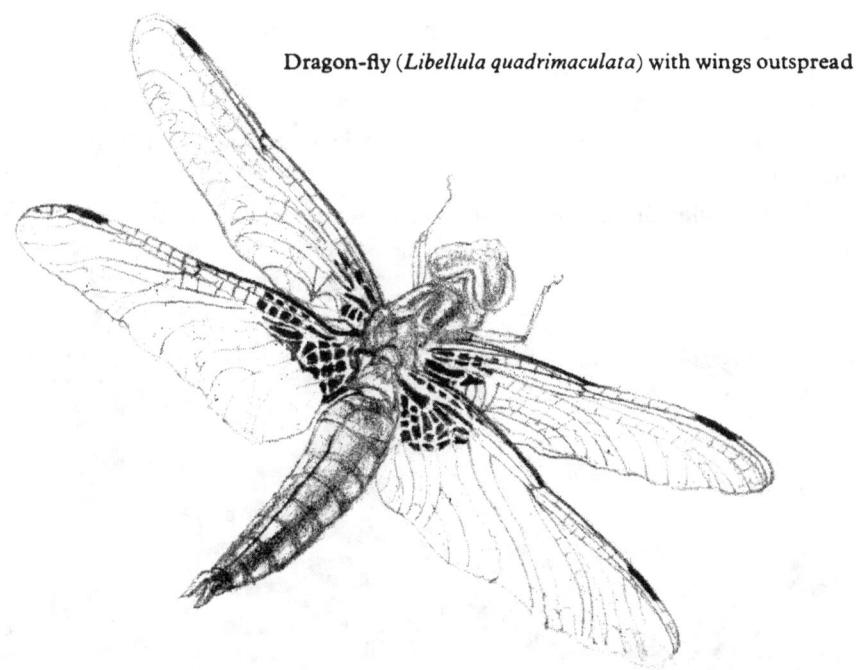

produce the vivid blue and green damsel-flies, 'Devil's Needles' that haunt the plants and grasses at the water's edge. The long brown ones are usually of the Aeshna group. They become quite tame in captivity, darting out from under a stone to take a piece of chopped worm from your fingers. These Aeshna nymphs crawl up rushes and reeds to undergo their metamorphosis. You must therefore house them in a container covered with a muslin tent tall enough to include growing reeds.

The leaf-like appendages at the end of the body are part of the nymph's breathing apparatus. This takes in water, filters from it the necessary oxygen and squirts out the surplus water, thus jet-propelling the nymph forward in a series of jerks. Its six legs enable it also to walk along the pond's bottom.

When drawing dragonflies, or any other insect, a point to remember

Nymphs of dragon-flies of the *Aeshna* group

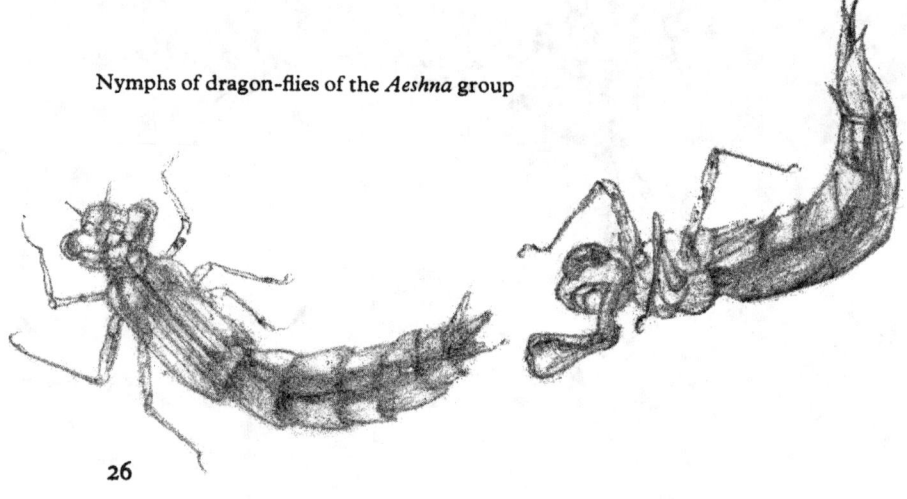

26

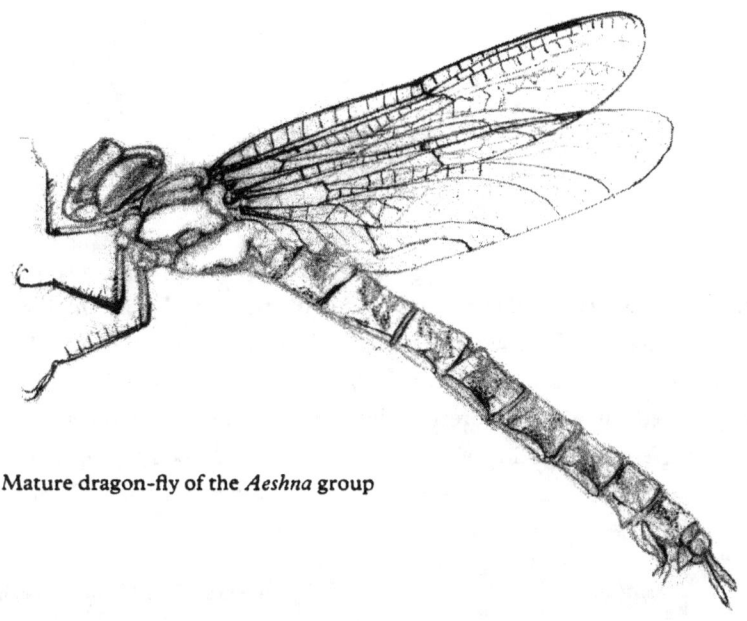

Mature dragon-fly of the *Aeshna* group

is that its construction differs from that of warm-blooded animals and birds, and from that of amphibians, snakes and lizards. An insect has no bones inside its body. It carries its skeleton outside, as a hard armour-plating, formed of a material called chitin. This shield covers the bodies of dragonflies, the body segments of bees and wasps, the middle part of the body of butterfly or moth, and it forms the hard wing-covers of beetles. The soft internal organs of insects are packed away inside their appointed places and cause no knots or ridges to influence the insect's clear outline.

# The pond in the forest

TODAY I WILL TAKE YOU to another pond. We will travel from the home
fields, through the fir wood, away across the heather, to the distant forest. A trackway leads us down to a peaty stream that winds between steep
fern-covered banks to the forest glades. There it widens out into a pond.
Weeds wave in the shallow water and stones make good hiding-places
for pond creatures, particularly in the shelter of a wooden bridge, beyond

Brown-speckled Stone-Loach

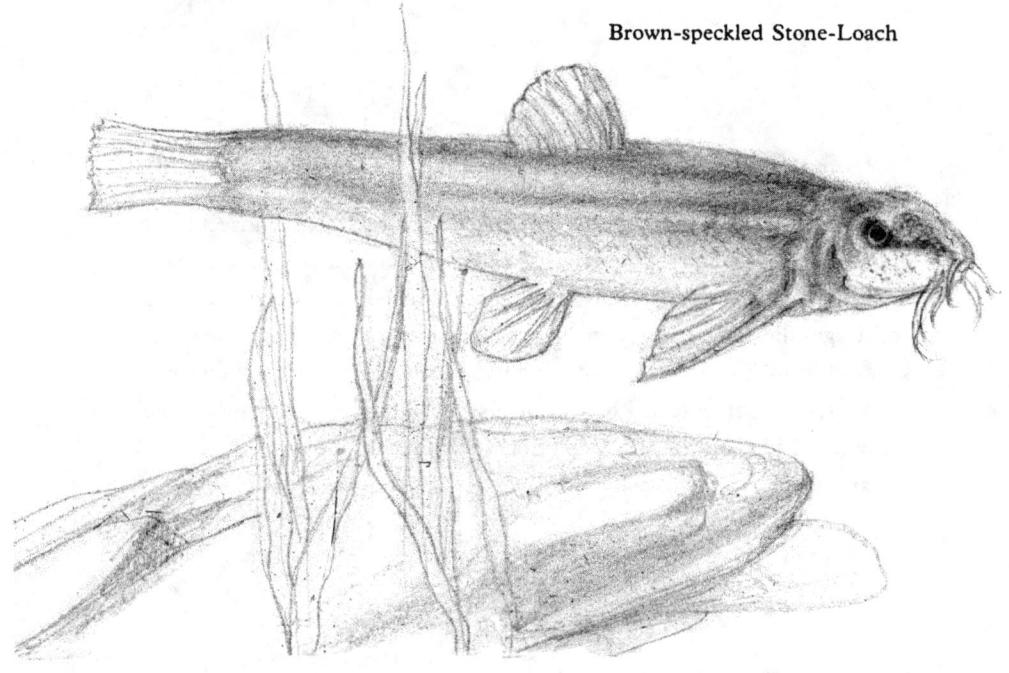

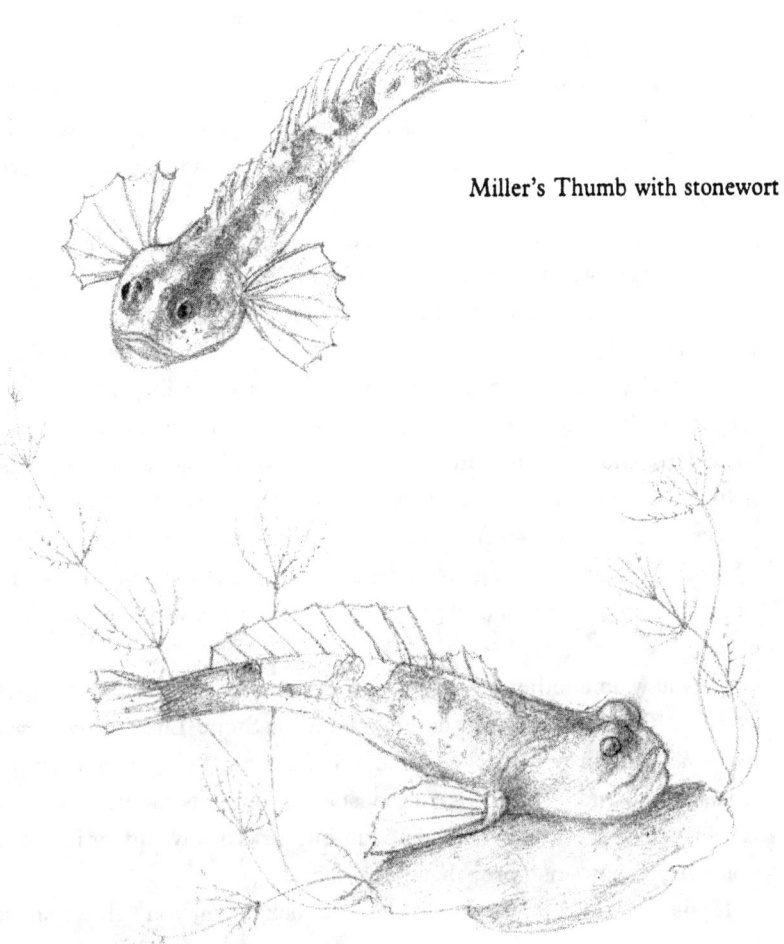

Miller's Thumb with stonewort

29

which the pond narrows once more into the stream following its intricate course through the forest.

Drag your net among the weeds, and in it you have that queer fish a Miller's Thumb (*Cottus gobio*). If you put it in a jam-pot of water, it will keep its head towards the glass perimeter, and you can study it, and even sketch it here.

Let us release it soon, for these inhabitants of moving streams soon die in the stagnant water of an aquarium. And there is nothing more impossible to draw than a dead fish; the living lines disappear, the colours fade, the fins close together. But the live creature has a beautiful sweep of line from the back of its head to the spread of its tail-fin. The Miller's Thumb is decorated with spines; the fins behind its head fan gracefully to and fro, and the light glints on the brown speckling of the body. The fish might have been blown out of one bubble of magical glass. Perhaps you could begin with several map-like drawings in order to get the proportion. Memory-drawings at home could be made in brown ink with a fine mapping pen, and a background of water-weeds would enhance the effect.

Do you want another fish of about the same size to draw on an opposite page? Turn over this big stone: under it is a Stone-Loach (*Nemacheilus barbatula*), brown-speckled like the Miller's Thumb but with a smaller head and a fringe, like a moustache, round its mouth. This also is a ground-fish; it doesn't swim about, but lurks always under its stone, pouncing on any small prey that comes along.

If you stand on the wooden bridge and look down, you will see shoals of small fish darting up and down stream. They are Minnows (*Phoxinus phoxinus*). Their colour is usually silvery-green with one dark stripe from head to tail; but in spring, during the courtship season, the males acquire vivid rainbow hues, wherewith to attract their females.

At a first glance, Minnows appear to be simple in shape. But when you begin to draw them you find that it is not as easy as it seems to make the drawings look alive. The widest part is apt to come in the wrong place, and the heads to be too big.

Three-spined Sticklebacks (*Gasterosteus aculeatus*) lurk here among this tangle of Canadian water-weed (*Elodea*). They have a distinctive and elegant shape, which is enhanced in the male by his iridiscent colouring, tinged with red.

Fish are ancient in their origins. Primitive fish inhabited the oceans of the Devonian period, hundreds of millions of years ago, and millions of years before plants and land creatures existed on our earth. Their fossils have been found imbedded in the old red sandstone which was laid down under these primordial seas. From the fish, newts have evolved: as you know they still spend part of their time in the water, though not in the sea.

There is, of course, no intermediate larval state in these fresh-water fish. Their eggs produce small fish, colourless and transparent, resembling their parents in shape and structure.

Weeds are a study in themselves. They should be carefully identified in the gently moving water. Most of them are rooted among the sand and pebbles of the bottom. But there is one unusual plant that I must

Pencil drawings of three-spined Stickleback
The male (below) is a handsome fish with iridescent colourings tinged with red;
at right is a female Stickleback exploring Canadian water-weed

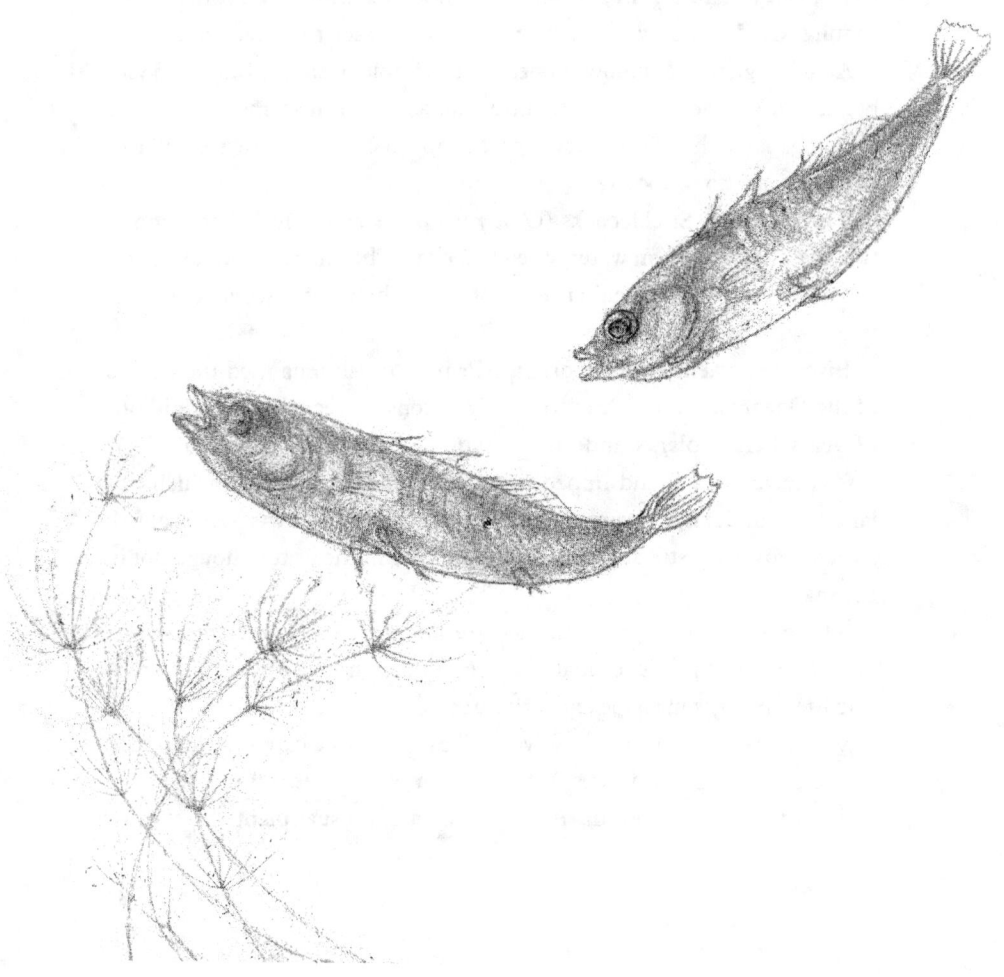

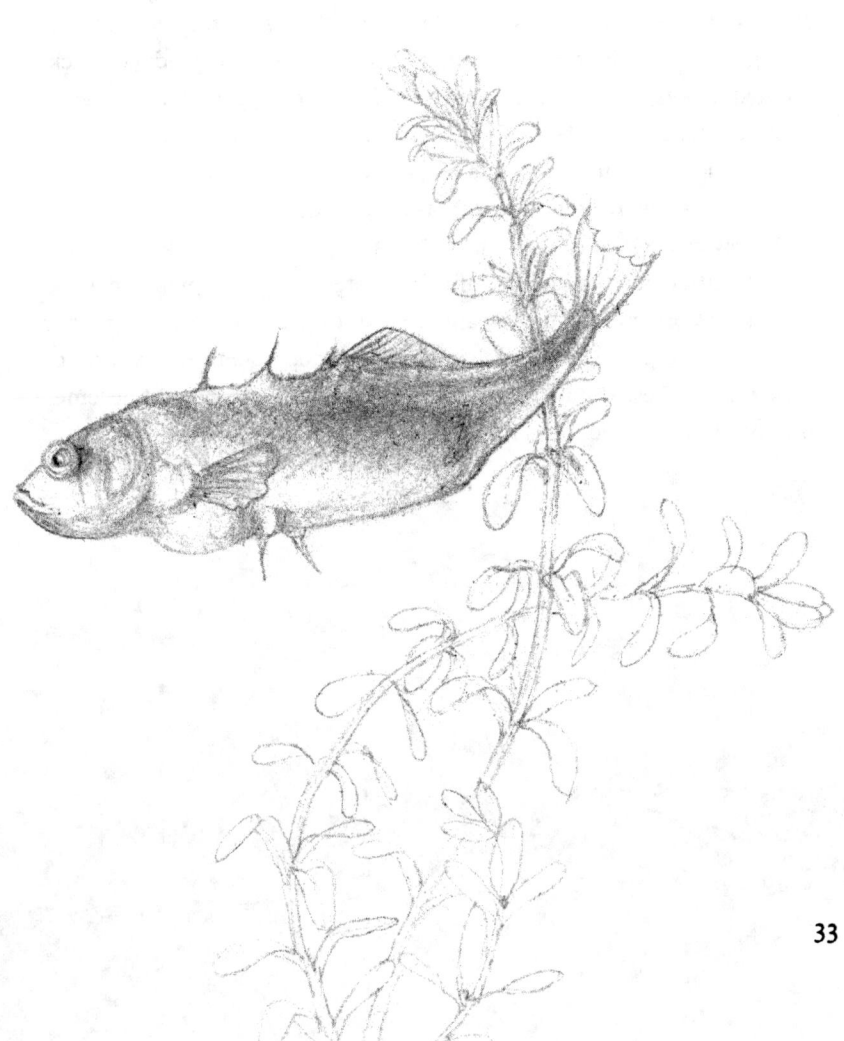

33

tell you about, for we cannot find it here. This is Frog-bit (*Hydrocharis morsus-ranae*), which has flat round leaves that float on the surface of the water, while the roots hang down into the water, but without ever taking root on the bottom. In autumn this curious weed produces thick, pointed shoots that break off and sink into the mud and sand—again without taking root. They lie until the spring; then they float to the surface and develop into new plants. Frog-bit will thrive in any shallow pan out-of-doors, where you can watch its cycle of growth.

Willow-moss (*Fontenalis*) is useful in an aquarium because of its neat growth. Often you may find a tuft of it rooted to a stone, which may be placed in a corner of the tank to afford cover to the small newts and other creatures. Stonewort (*Chara*) has long internodes between whorls of dark green spikes. If lime is present in the water, the stonewort becomes encrusted with it, and looks rather like coral.

Water-crowfoot

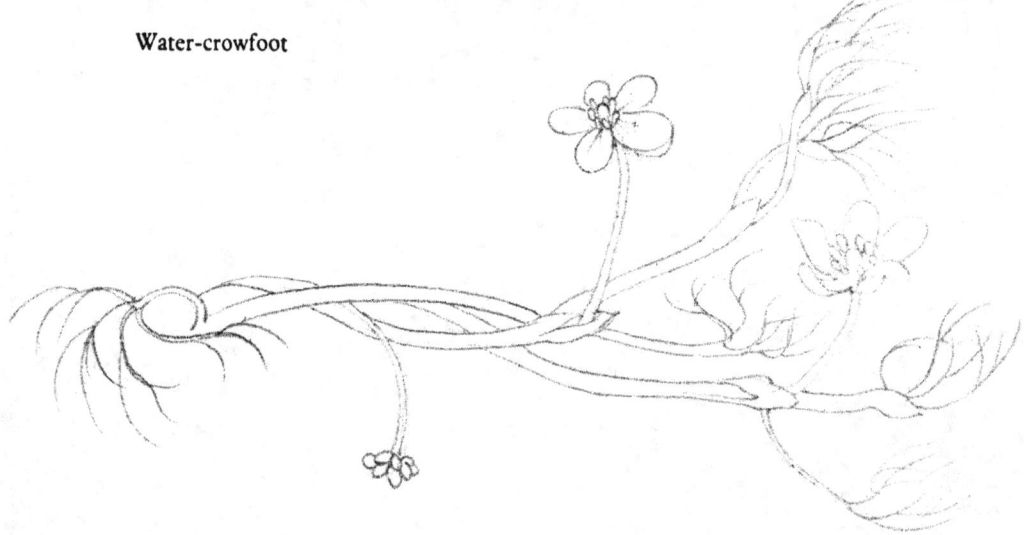

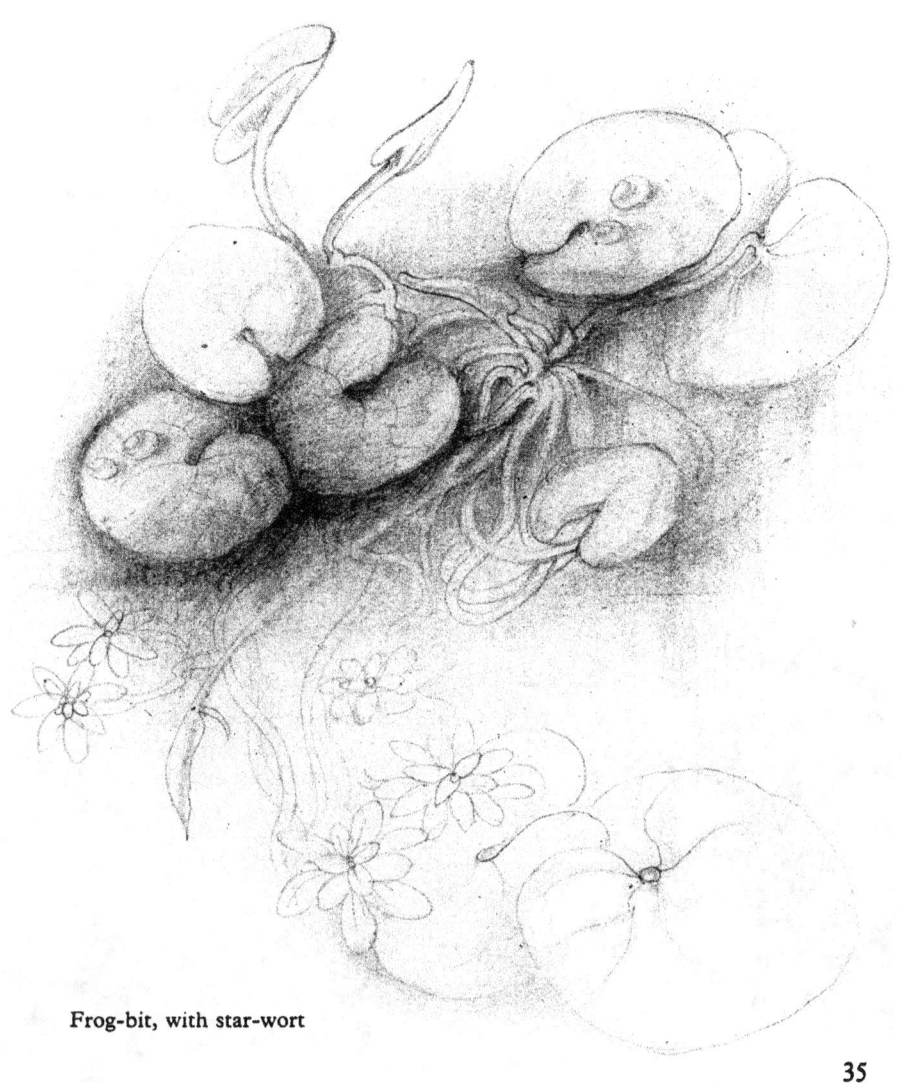

Frog-bit, with star-wort

35

Dredge up this mass of mixed weeds, and in it you will find a Water-scorpion (*Nepa cinerea*) and a number of Water-boatmen (*Notonecta glanca*). Both are allied to bugs and belong to the order Hemiptera. These species thrive in an aquarium, but do not put the Boatmen in a tank in company with a Great Crested Newt. He will stalk them with the slow stealthy movements of a cat stalking a bird. A dart of his head, and the Boatman is swallowed at a gulp. If he misses his kill, he may tear off one of the long fringed hind-legs, and the Boatman, unable to swim or feed, will perish miserably.

These two species live in and under the water, sucking juices with their beak-like mouths which give a bird-like look to the immature

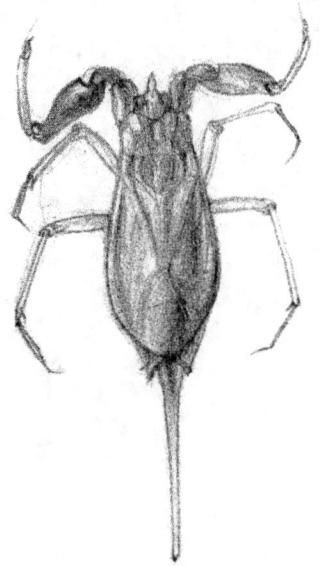

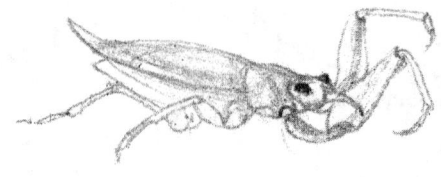

Pencil drawing of a Water-Scorpion with its nymph.
The protruding beak of
the latter gives it a curiously bird-like look

Water-boatmen, another
species of aquatic bug living in and
under the water

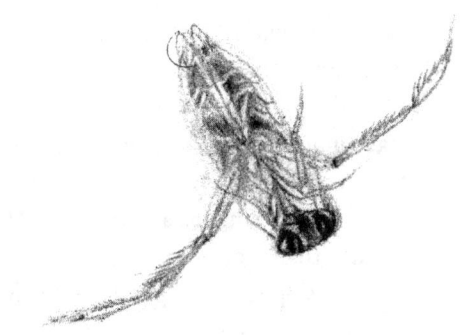

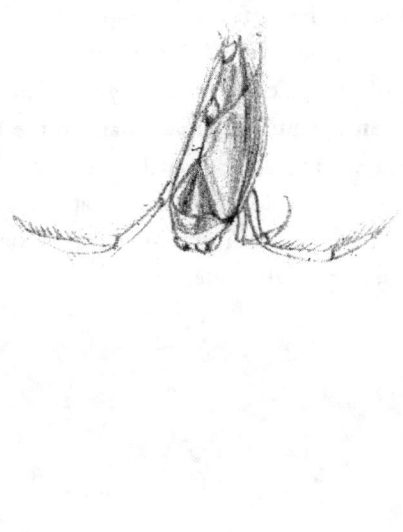

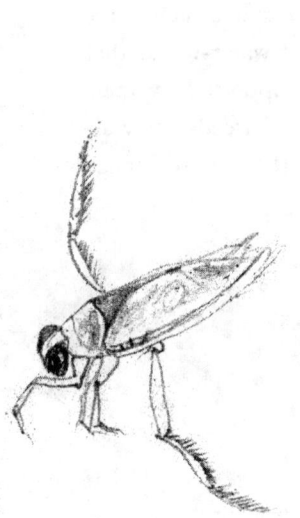

37

Water-scorpion. But there is an allied Aquatic Bug (*Gerris*), occurring in numbers on the lower reach of this pond, which slides about on the surface of the water. These pond-skaters are slender with immensely long legs, difficult to see as they dart from sun into shade, and still more difficult to catch.

There is a smaller aquatic bug, *Hydrmetza*, the Water Measurer, so slender that it suggests a knotted wisp of black thread. The Measurer frequents open sunny ponds in the meadows or on moors, where it darts to and fro on the surface of the water as if it were measuring the area. These Skaters and Measurers are able to walk on the water because of the elasticity of its surface film (if you stand by the side of your aquarium and bring your eye to the level of the top of the water you may see a beetle, or a fish, push up the surface film which stretches upwards, tent-wise, without breaking). The surface film supports flat floating leaves such as those of the Frog-bit, while the water below, by its density supports the spread branches of the tufted or trailing types of plant. Stiff stems such as are borne by land plants are unnecessary to the buoyant water-weeds that can spread their flexible branches, sheltered and supported by their watery element. You will observe that the submerged weeds show always small, finely cut, or grass-like leaves that offer the least resistance to the movement of the water.

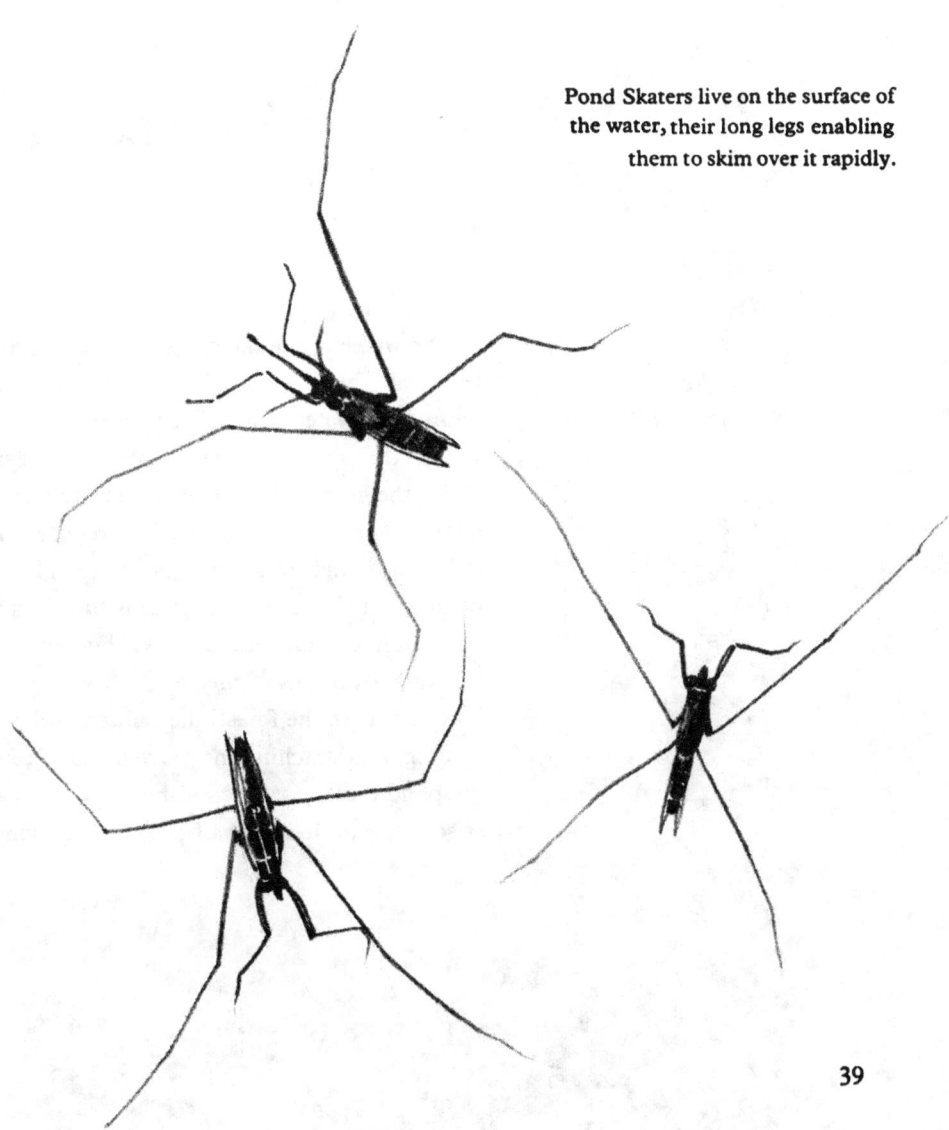

Pond Skaters live on the surface of
the water, their long legs enabling
them to skim over it rapidly.

39

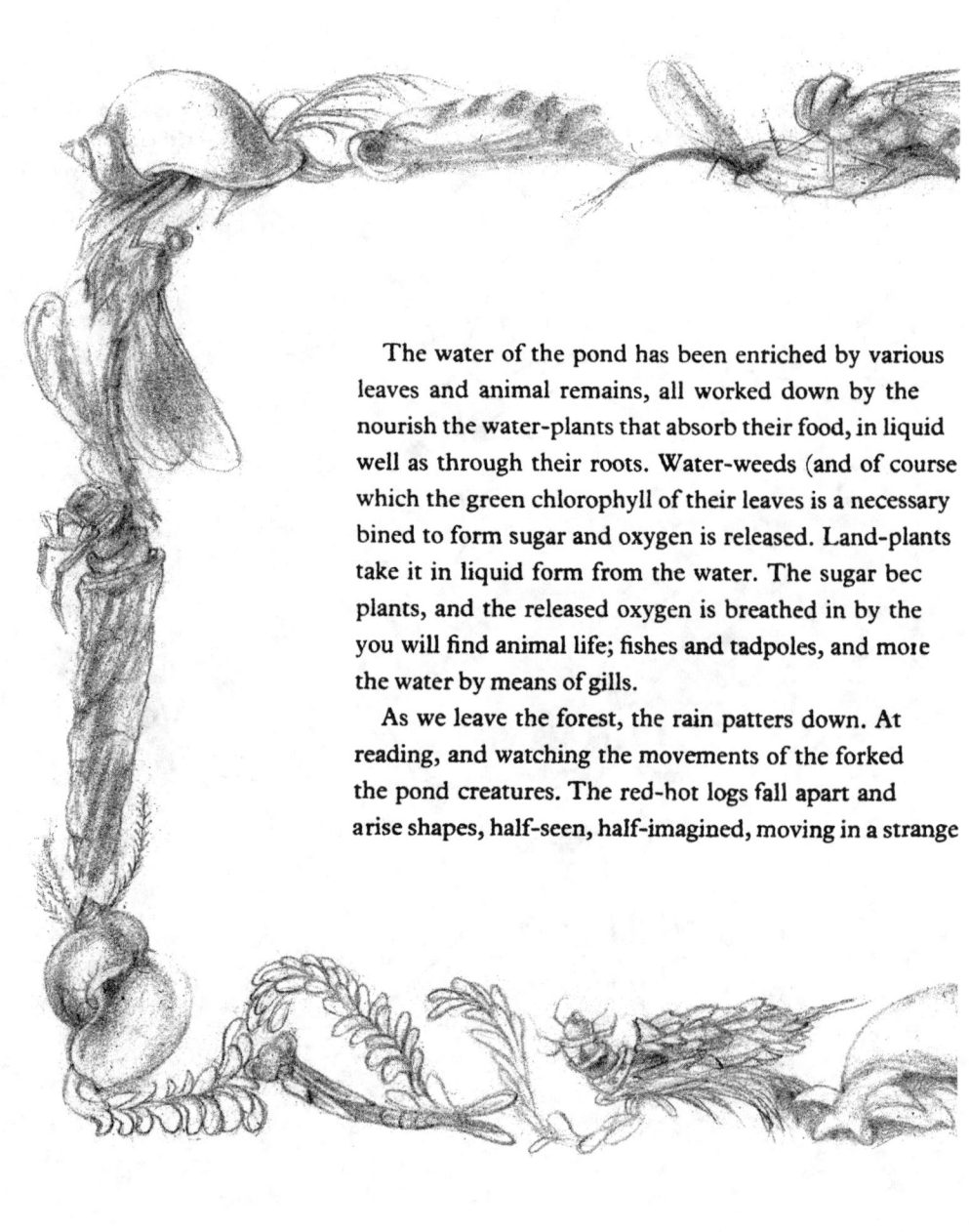

The water of the pond has been enriched by various leaves and animal remains, all worked down by the nourish the water-plants that absorb their food, in liquid well as through their roots. Water-weeds (and of course which the green chlorophyll of their leaves is a necessary bined to form sugar and oxygen is released. Land-plants take it in liquid form from the water. The sugar bec plants, and the released oxygen is breathed in by the you will find animal life; fishes and tadpoles, and more the water by means of gills.

As we leave the forest, the rain patters down. At reading, and watching the movements of the forked the pond creatures. The red-hot logs fall apart and arise shapes, half-seen, half-imagined, moving in a strange

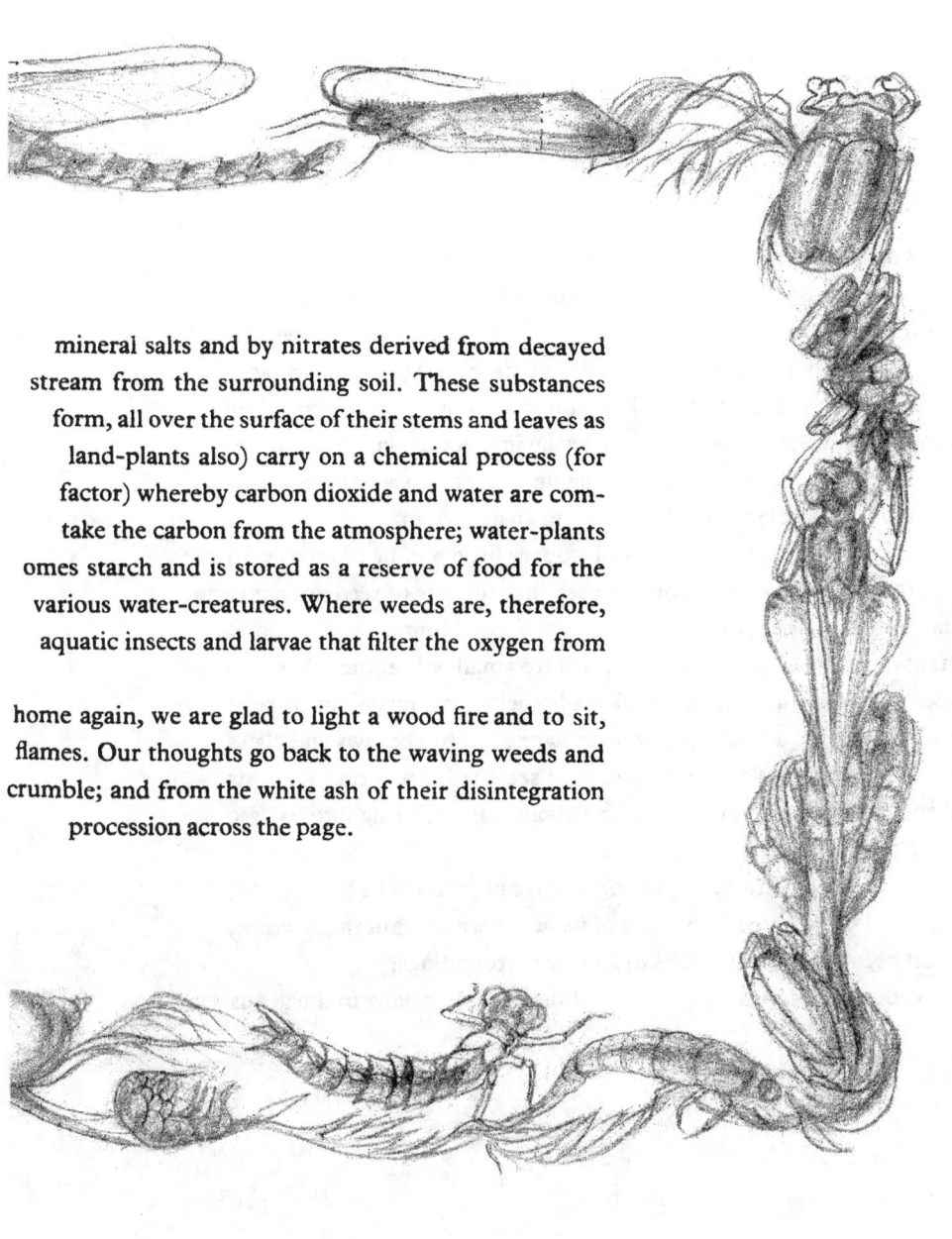

mineral salts and by nitrates derived from decayed
stream from the surrounding soil. These substances
form, all over the surface of their stems and leaves as
land-plants also) carry on a chemical process (for
factor) whereby carbon dioxide and water are com-
take the carbon from the atmosphere; water-plants
omes starch and is stored as a reserve of food for the
various water-creatures. Where weeds are, therefore,
aquatic insects and larvae that filter the oxygen from

home again, we are glad to light a wood fire and to sit,
flames. Our thoughts go back to the waving weeds and
crumble; and from the white ash of their disintegration
procession across the page.

# Odd shapes

WHEN YOU DREDGE through the mud and weeds in a pond, you may find in your net an assortment of small, odd shapes. The hopping Water-shrimps (*Gammarus*) arrest your attention first. They appear to be ugly little creatures; but if you put them for the time being into a jam jar of water and watch them through a lens you will observe the structure and movements of these crustaceans as they swim about, sometimes upside down, with the hind pair of legs trailing up over the back. These Water-shrimps invariably die after a day or two in an aquarium.

Then you may pick out of the mud a queer little bundle of reeds with the short ends sticking out. You then see that the bits of reed are cut to the same length, like sawn logs, and superimposed round a central core, and that there is a large hole at one end and a small hole at the other; and you perceive that this bundle is in fact a home; a most ingenious piece of insect architecture, a house built not by hands but by the jaws and claws of the inhabitant. If you watch you may see the larva thrust forth its head and two pairs of legs, so crawling about but retreating into its case should danger threaten.

If placed in an aquarium containing weeds not found in its home pond, a caddis will redecorate the exterior of its house with bits of these weeds, so that it becomes inconspicuous in its new surroundings.

The caddis that construct these reed-bundle cases belong to the genus

Pencil drawings of Water Shrimps,
generally found in the mud and weeds at the bottom of a pond

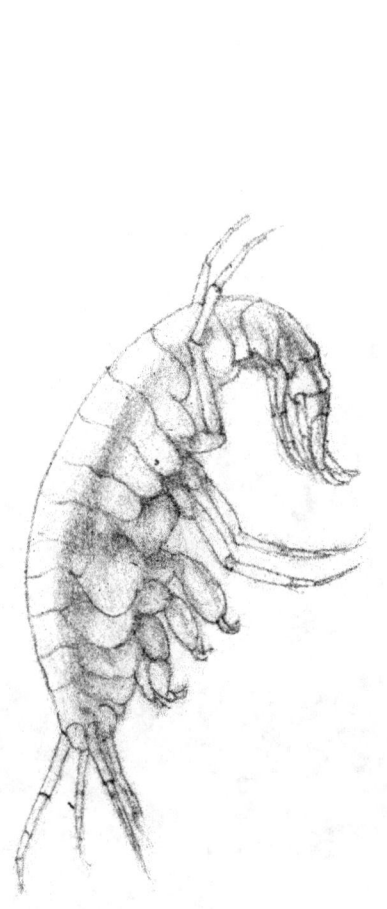
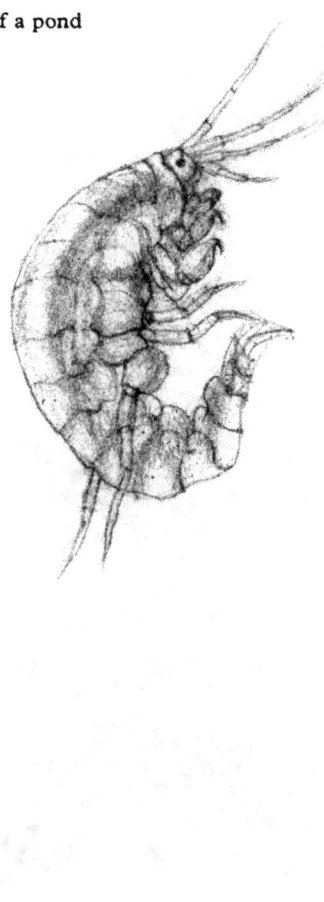

43

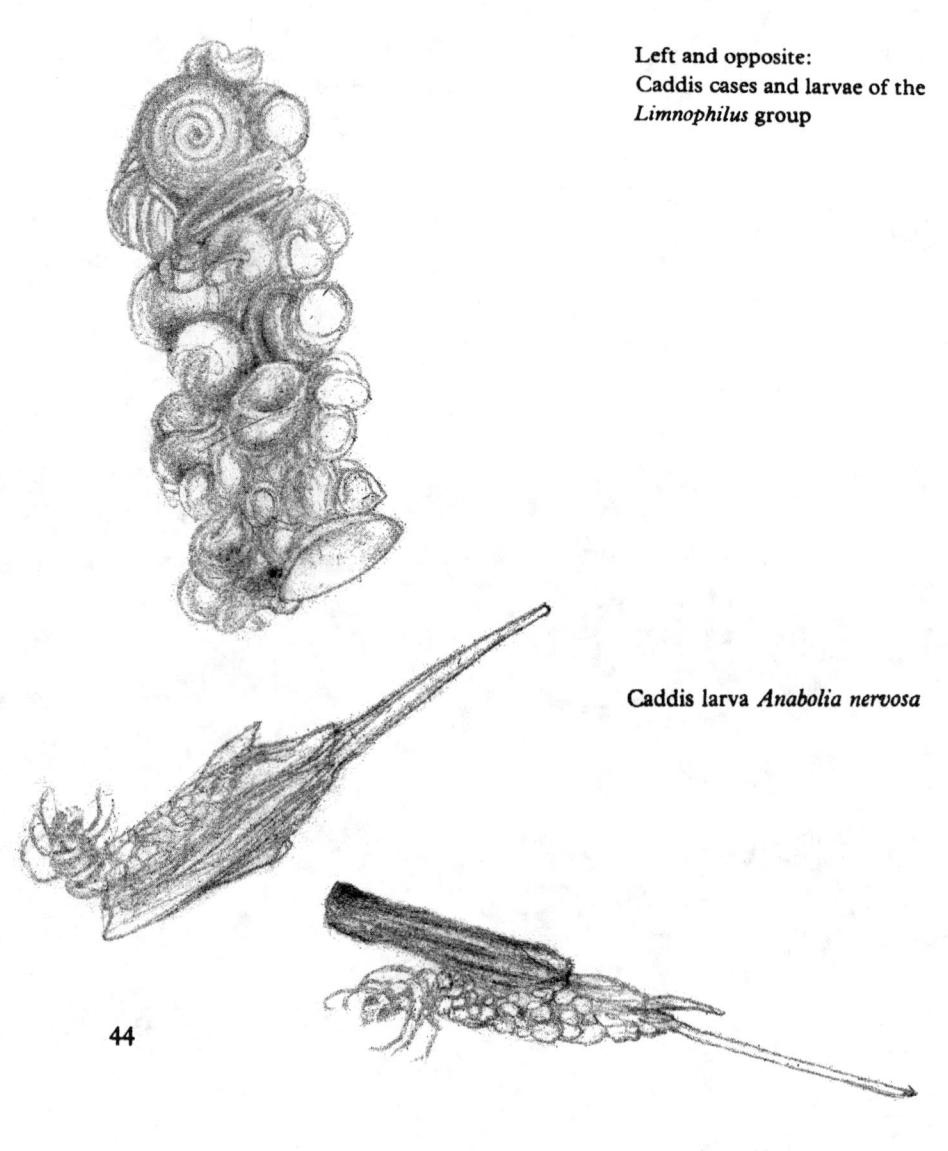

Left and opposite:
Caddis cases and larvae of the
*Limnophilus* group

Caddis larva *Anabolia nervosa*

44

*Limnophilus* of the order Trichoptera. Other species, inhabiting streams or ponds, build cases of sticks, pebbles, grains of sand and even of small freshwater-snails.

In due course, after sealing its door, the larva changes into a pupa; and

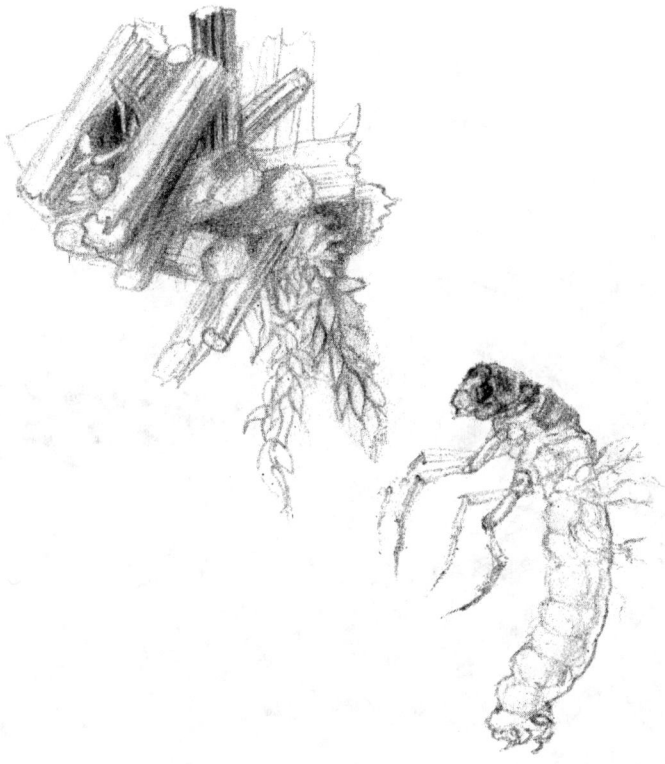

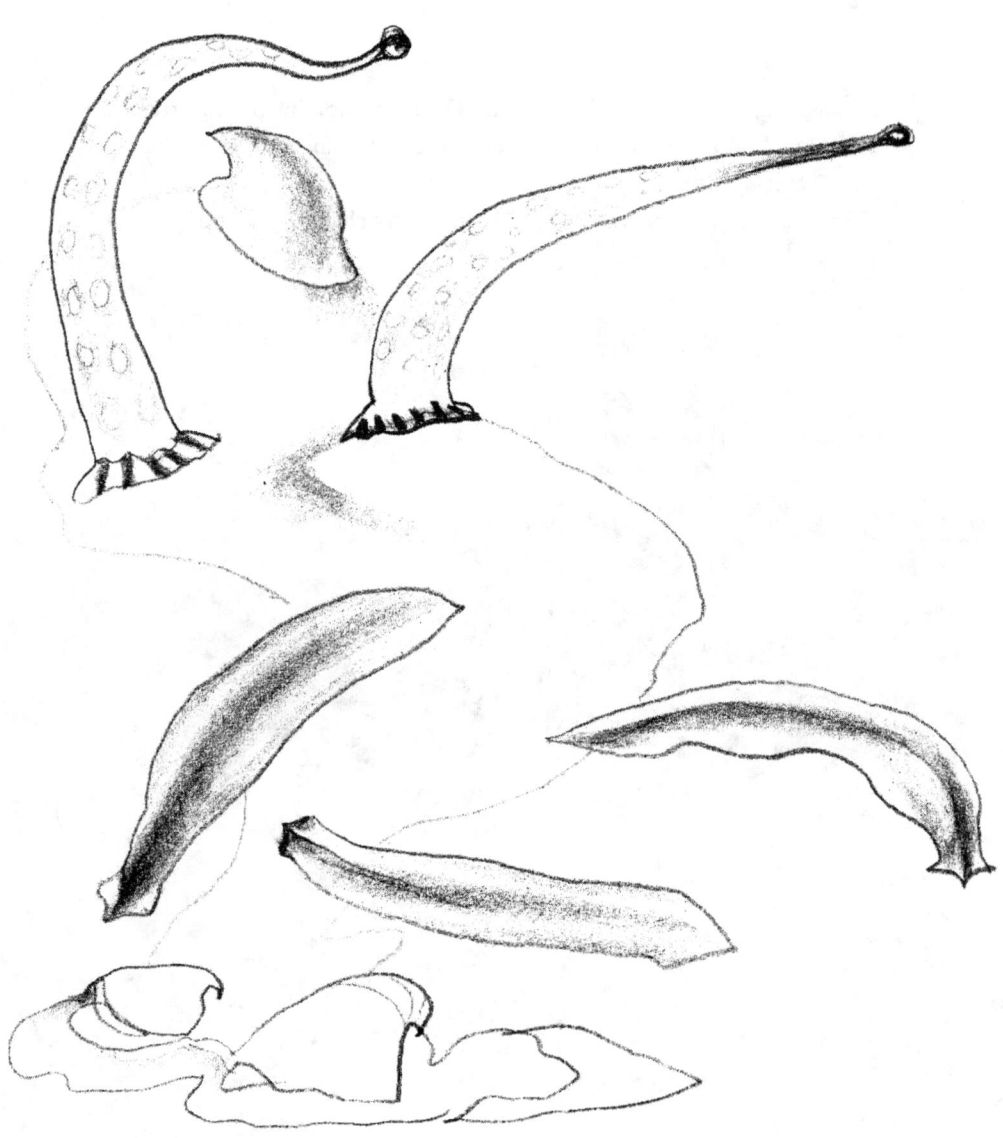

Rapid sketches of Hydra with
Daphnia opposite:
Leeches, Limpets and Flatworms

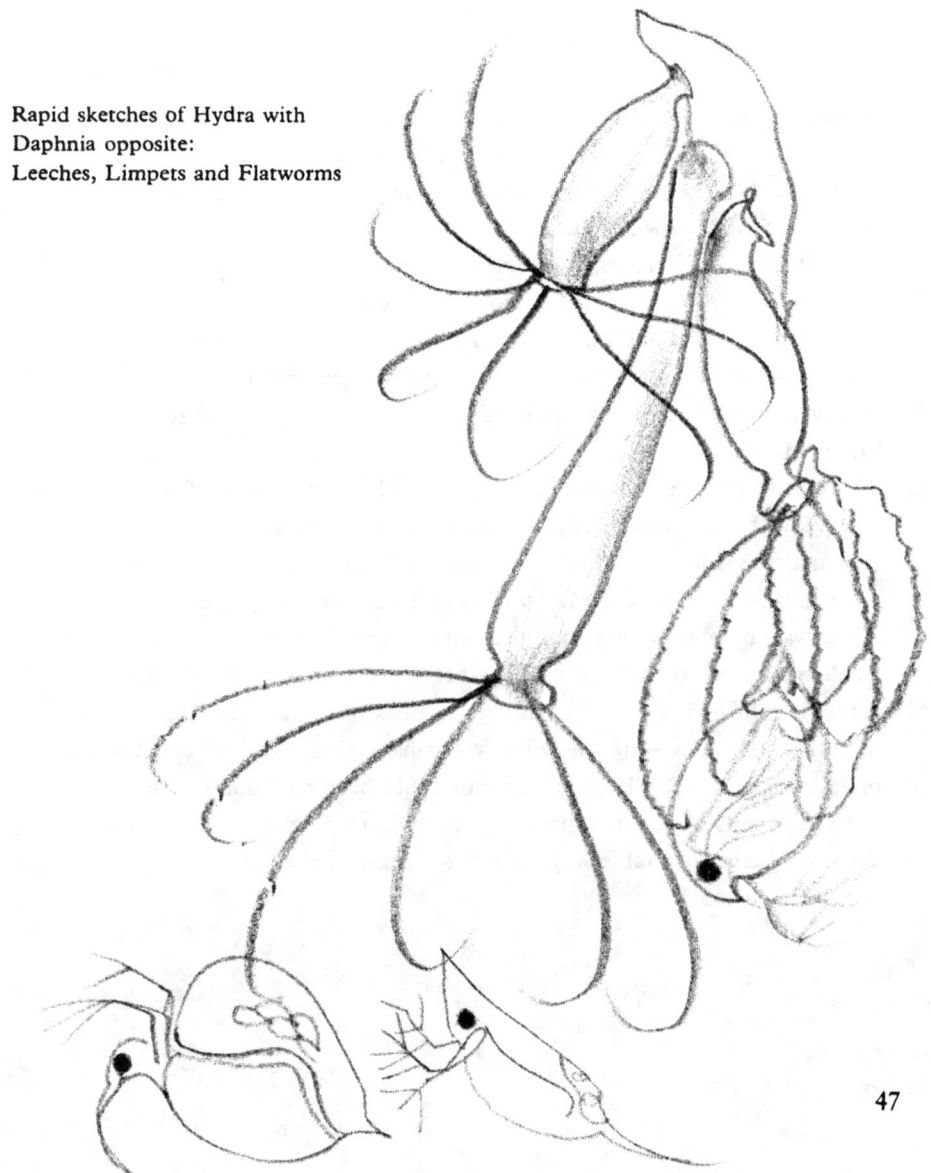

47

by and by the fragile, long-winged caddis fly emerges to complete the cycle and to lay eggs over or in the water. Sometimes, when you walk by a pond or stream, these caddis-flies rise in swarms from the grasses and scatter like wind-blown chaff.

Small shreds of black rubber cling to these pebbles in your net— place them in a bowl of water and leave them there till the evening, when they elongate and move and take shape as flatworms (Planarians), neatly shaped and sometimes patterned. These creatures are free-living relatives of parasitic worms that inhabit the internal organs of sheep and other animals.

And here are two lumps of green jelly sticking to a frond of water-weed. Put them, weed and all, in a tumbler of water in the light, and the jelly-masses gradually open like sea-anemones (to which they are related) waving a halo of green tentacles. These hydras are hungry creatures. Their waving tentacles are equipped with stinging cells that poison any small living creature that comes in contact with them. The tentacles close round it and the hydra feeds. Its diet consists principally of Daphnia, minute crustaceans—the so-called water-fleas that are, perhaps, the oddest shapes of all. These small forms could be spaced out on a large sheet of paper and drawn in brown, pink, and green chalk to form a design for curtains, or a tablecloth, or a child's dress.

# The pond by the sea

THE POND BY THE SEA lies on the landward side of the sand-dunes that form a barrier between the shore and the heath. On stormy days, the waters of this mere take on the changing colours of the ocean itself; yet these waters are neither salt, nor brackish; they are sweet, and harbour an immense number of freshwater creatures.

There are spider-like nymphs of the *Sympetrum* group, of which some species produce scarlet dragonflies, and slender nymphs of damsel-flies. Caddis creep among the weeds, and now and then you may see a Water-spider. In a little bay Whirligig Beetles (*Gyrinus natator*) dither about, each with its air-bubble. Great Diving Beetles (*Dytiscus marginalis*) haunt the deeper water.

Water-beetles must breathe air; accordingly they come up to the surface from time to time to take in a fresh supply, which they store in the space between the body and the wing-covers and among hairs to which bubbles adhere. I have often watched a Great Diving Beetle resting upside down below the water of an aquarium, with the tip of its abdomen thrusting through the surface film into the fresh air.

Beetles have a hard texture, with a sharp silhouette and quick movements. These are best translated into a drawing by using a pointed brush filled with monochrome black or sepia, thickened with Chinese white.

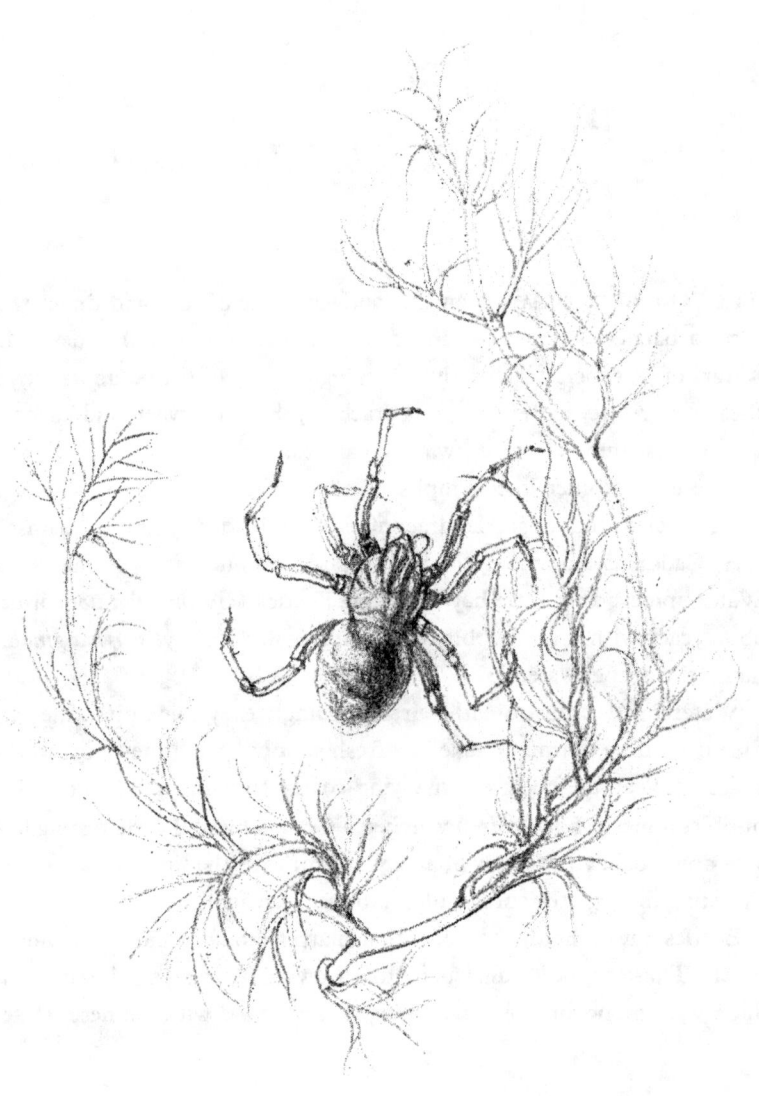

Pencil drawings of a nymph of a dragon-fly
of the *Sympetrum* group and,
opposite, a Water-Spider

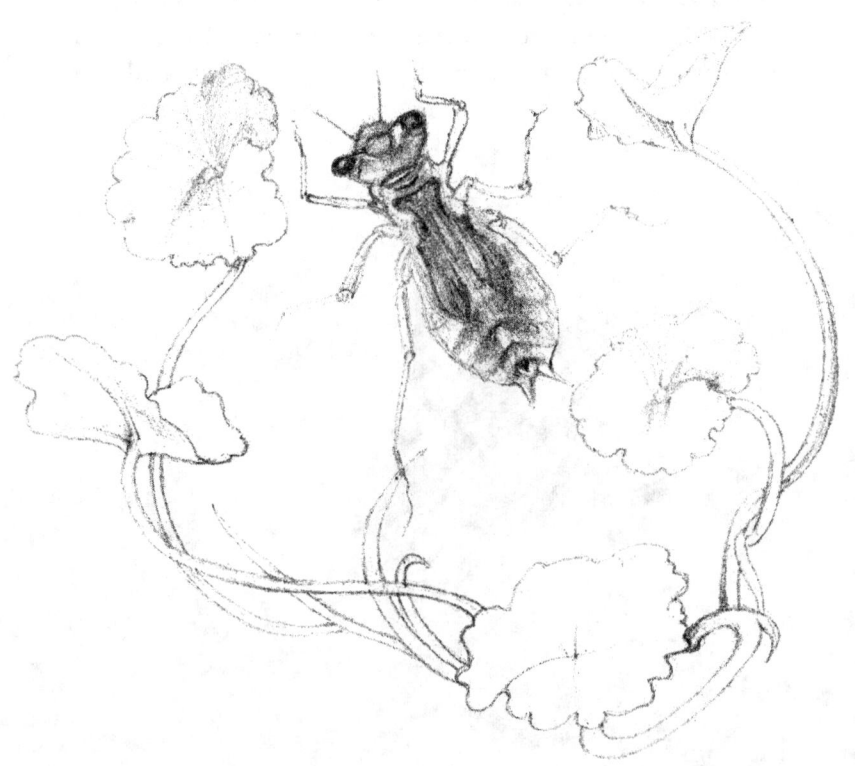

The pointed brush gives a swift line. Previous experience with pencil drawings will help you to use the brush with speed and decision. When making an elaborate design, you may paint the beetle first, in detail; this gives the key to the weight of the rest of the design, which is subsidiary and so placed as to direct attention to the insect itself. From mono-chrome studies, it is but a step to the use of colour. For coloured pictures of beetles and other insects I use a dead-white, smooth-surfaced paper,

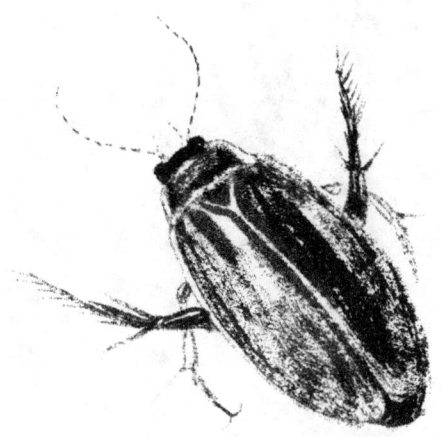

or Japanese or Chinese paper. The success of a painting depends largely upon the suitability of the paper for the medium used.

You may make a handwritten, illustrated journal of your pond work, spacing out the manuscript notes so that they form part of the design of the page by balancing the drawings. The fifteenth and sixteenth century Dutch and Italian artists combined calligraphy and draughtsmanship in this way in their letters and notebooks with most pleasing effect.

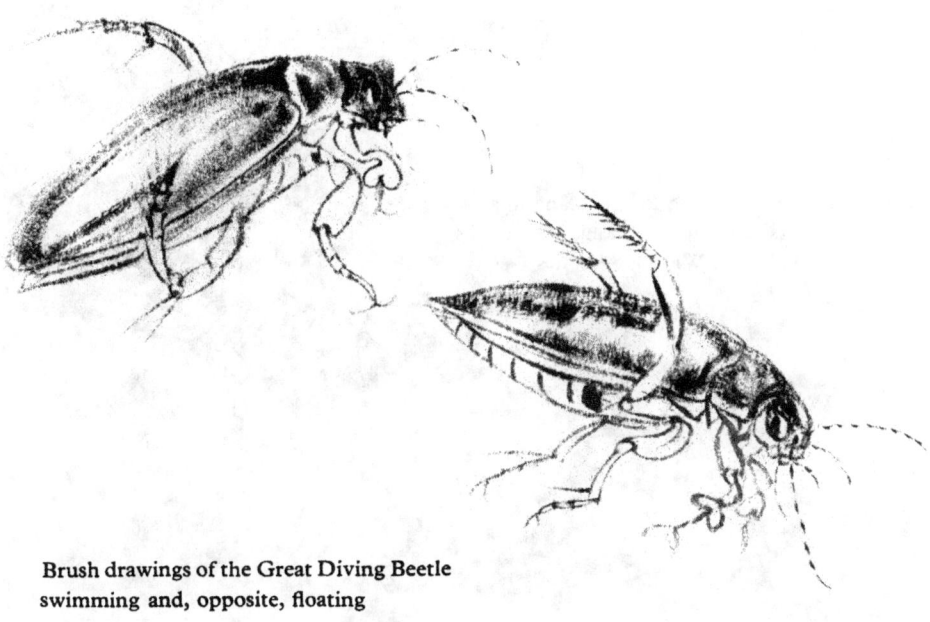

Brush drawings of the Great Diving Beetle swimming and, opposite, floating

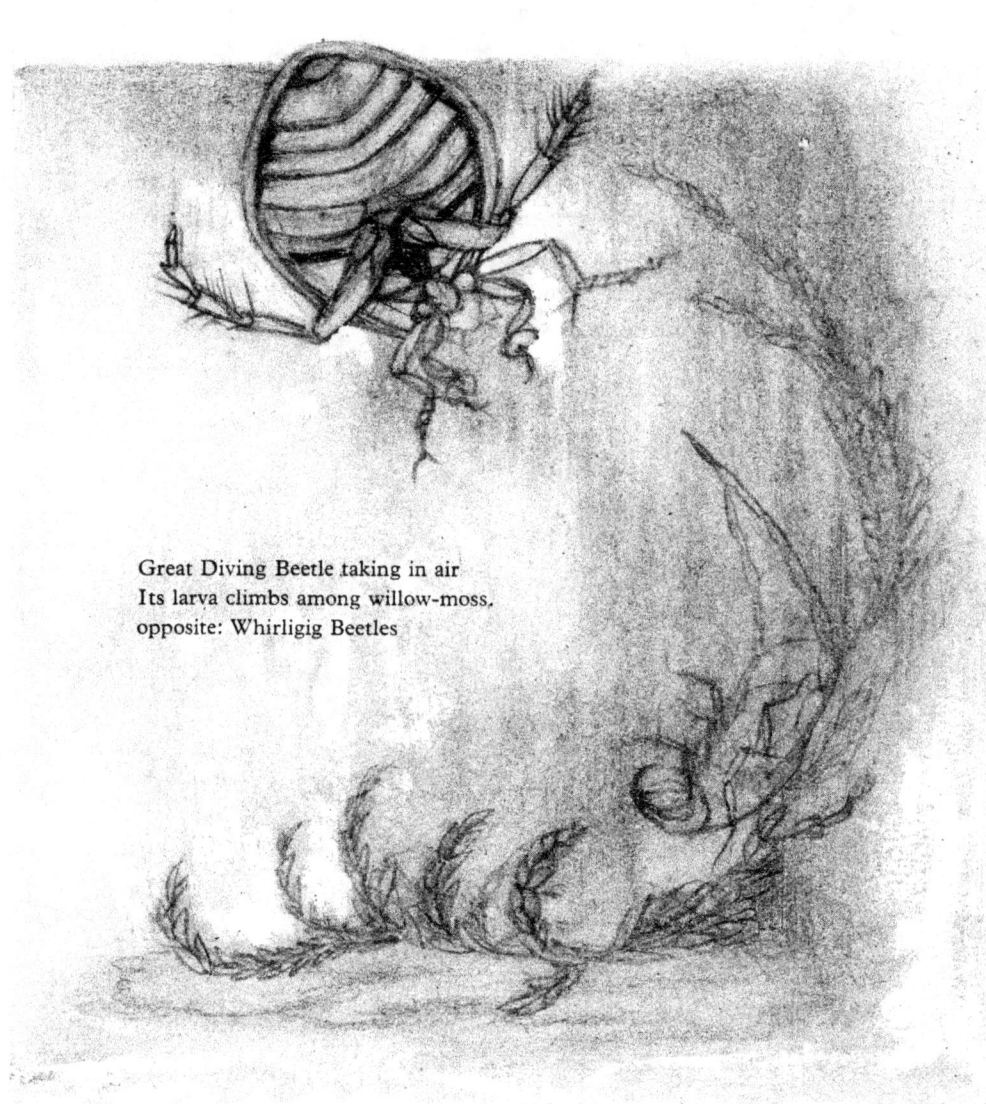

Great Diving Beetle taking in air
Its larva climbs among willow-moss.
opposite: Whirligig Beetles

You will see the suggested arrangement in my sketch of the Water Beetle taking in air opposite.

The larva of the Great Diving Beetle is long, thin and fierce. When fully grown it leaves the water and pupates in the earth of the pond bank. If you find a larva you must house it in a vessel of water placed inside a larger container, the space between the two being stuffed with earth. Place over all a large sheet of butter-muslin tied firmly round and under the outer vessel. Two lengths of wire or cane bent into hoops serve as a support for the muslin. Place them at right angles to each other, tie them where they cross at the centre, and push the ends into the earth between the two containers. By this arrangement the larva has light, space and a more or less natural environment, and it cannot escape.

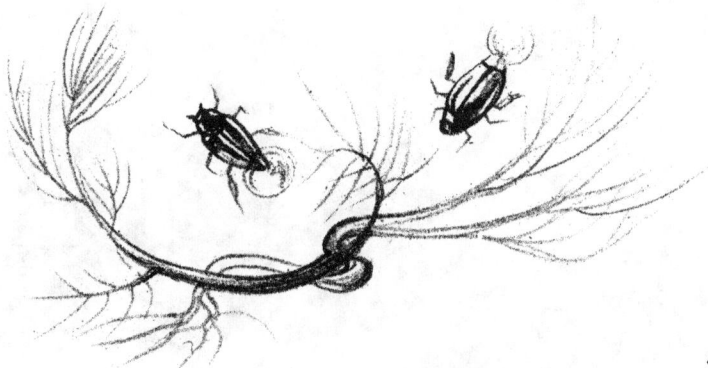

Freshwater snails are also good subjects for wash drawings—but the apparent simplicity of their beautiful curves is deceptive; it is not easy to achieve a drawing of these spiral forms, nor to observe accurately the shape of the curious creature that unfolds and extends from within the shell. The front part of the body appears first, with two sensory tentacles. In the Great Pond Snail (*Limnea stagnalis*) these are flat and triangular. In the Freshwater Winkle (*Viviparus viviparus*) they are threadlike. There is an eye at the base of each tentacle and a mouth underneath. The lower part of the body is called the foot, and the internal organs lie

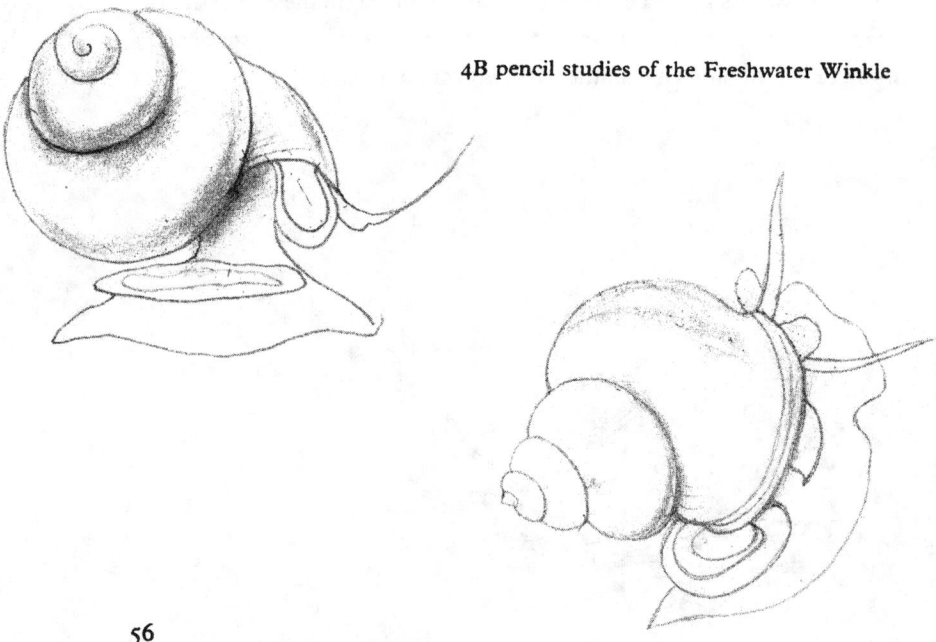

4B pencil studies of the Freshwater Winkle

56

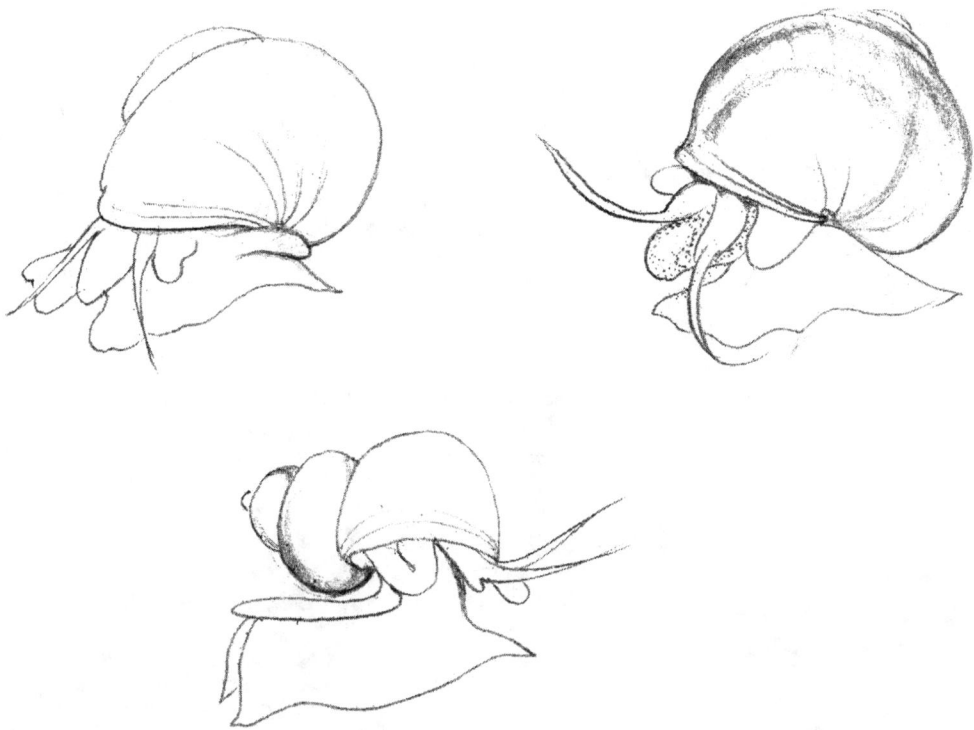

in the part of the body hidden by the shell, to which it is attached by muscles.

Snails move at night. If you put a light at the back of your aquarium you will be entranced by their gliding movements among weeds and over rocks and stones.

Freshwater snails are divided into two groups, the operculates (of

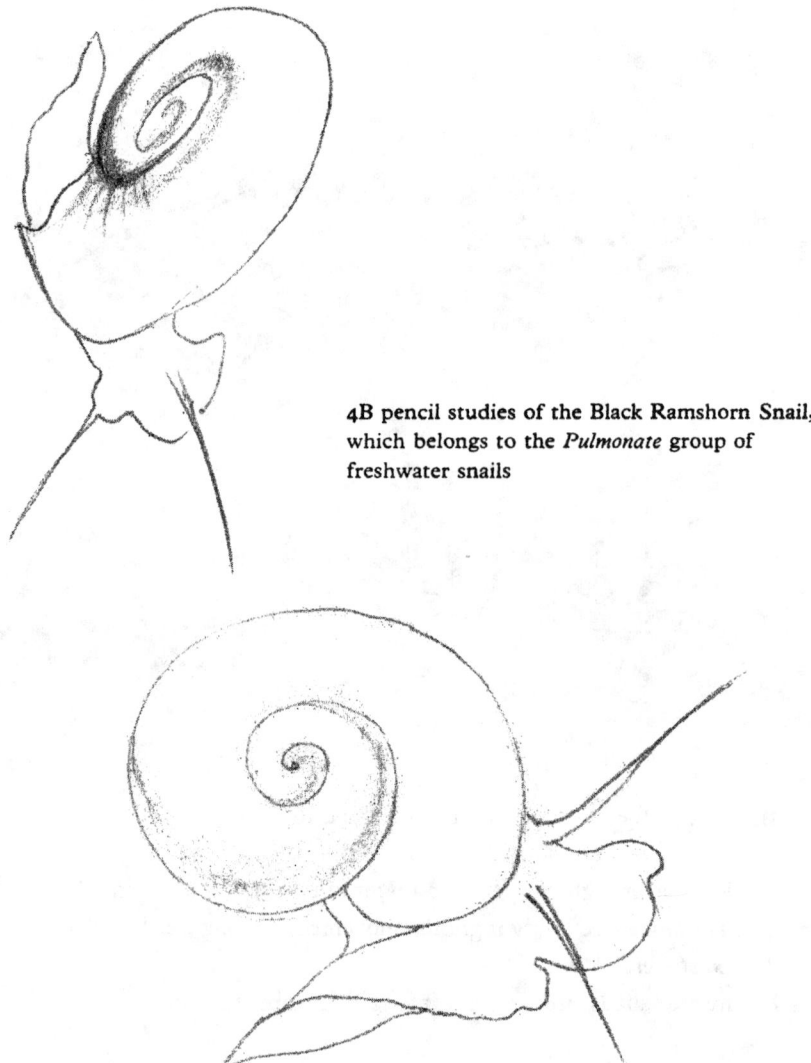

4B pencil studies of the Black Ramshorn Snail,
which belongs to the *Pulmonate* group of
freshwater snails

58

which the Winkle is one) and the pulmonates comprising the Great Pond Snail, the Ramshorn Snail (*Planorbis corneus*) and many others. The operculates breathe air filtered from the water by means of their gills; they have a flat horny plate attached to the end of their body with which they can close the shell's entrance. The female Winkle produces living young, and the sexes in the group are distinct. Pulmonate snails breathe air and rise to the water's surface to take it into their lung. Each individual pulmonate snail contains male and female organs, and every one therefore is capable of laying eggs, which may sometimes be found in

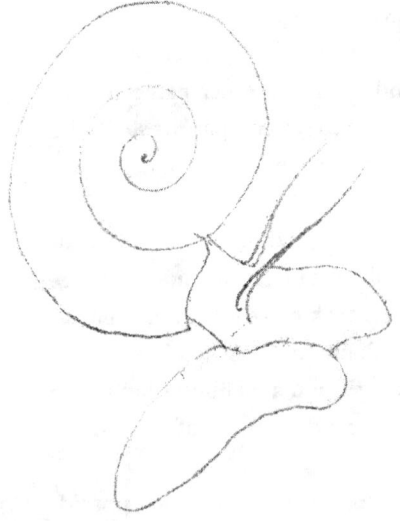

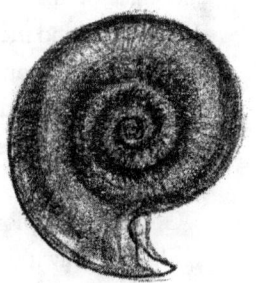

jelly-like masses among the weeds. In his book *Freshwater Life of the British Isles* John Clegg tells us that these pulmonates are thought to be descended from a group of land snails which returned to the water—but freshwater snails, taken as a whole, are descended from the snails of the salt sea. The sea is the cradle of all life, and in it, in long ages past, in the Jurassic period, lived the large flat spiral shells that have become fossilised as ammonites. There were small freshwater snails living too, at that time, or a little later, in estuaries and marshes. As the seas receded and the landscape changed, more snails gradually found their way up estuaries and rivers into ponds, which many kinds found to their liking, remaining there and settling down and eventually producing the variously shaped shells that we find today; whilst others migrated on to dry land to form our great company of land snails. Another name for the Great Pond Snail is the Freshwater Whelk. You can compare its shell with that of the sea whelks lying on the tideline, on the shore, a long stone's throw from the mere.

The water plants, and land plants also, are descended from the weeds and algae of ancient seas, which had perforce to migrate and to change their shapes and methods of reproducing their kind as more land-masses took shape. So you see that in studying Pond Life you will have under your eyes, constantly, a reminder of past ages and a manifestation of the extraordinary shapes that have arisen during the course of the earth's history.

Go now to explore other ponds and meres. I have left much unsaid, nor have I drawn for you more than a few of the creatures to be found in ponds. You will find others. Perhaps you will wander down the river, and the estuary, and find your way to mountain torrents and moorland streams. Water has its own magic, that soothes the senses and awakens the imagination; and I can think of no better preparation for a spell of work than to rest among the heather with the mere beneath us, and in our ears the sound of the sea.

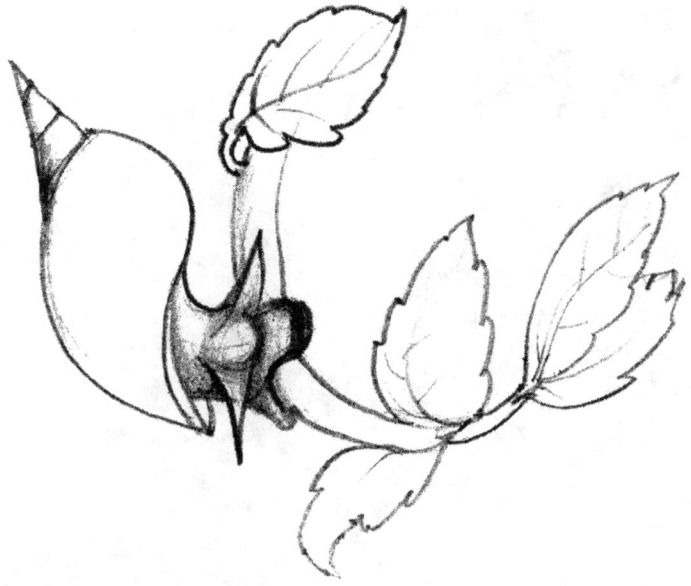

Eared Pond Snail shell on pond cress

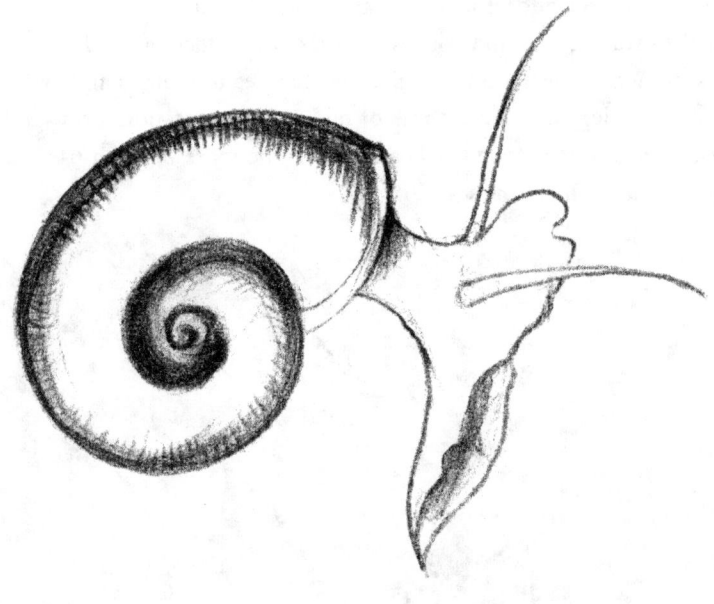

Red Ramshorn Snail

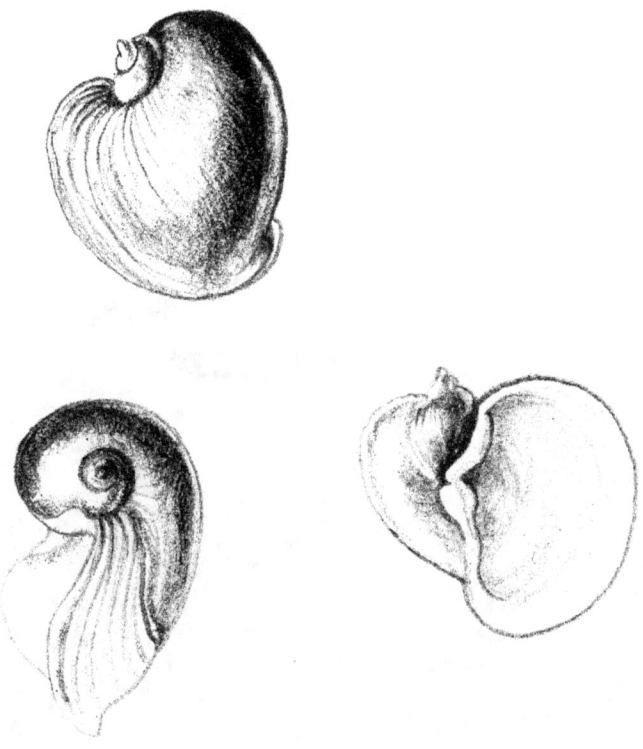

Ear Snail

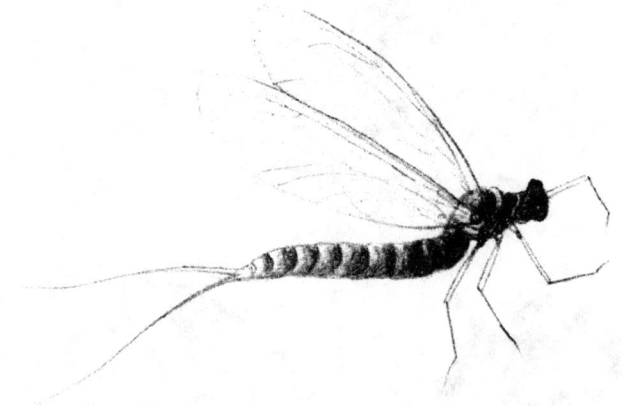

64

# Coachwhip Publications

### CoachwhipBooks.com

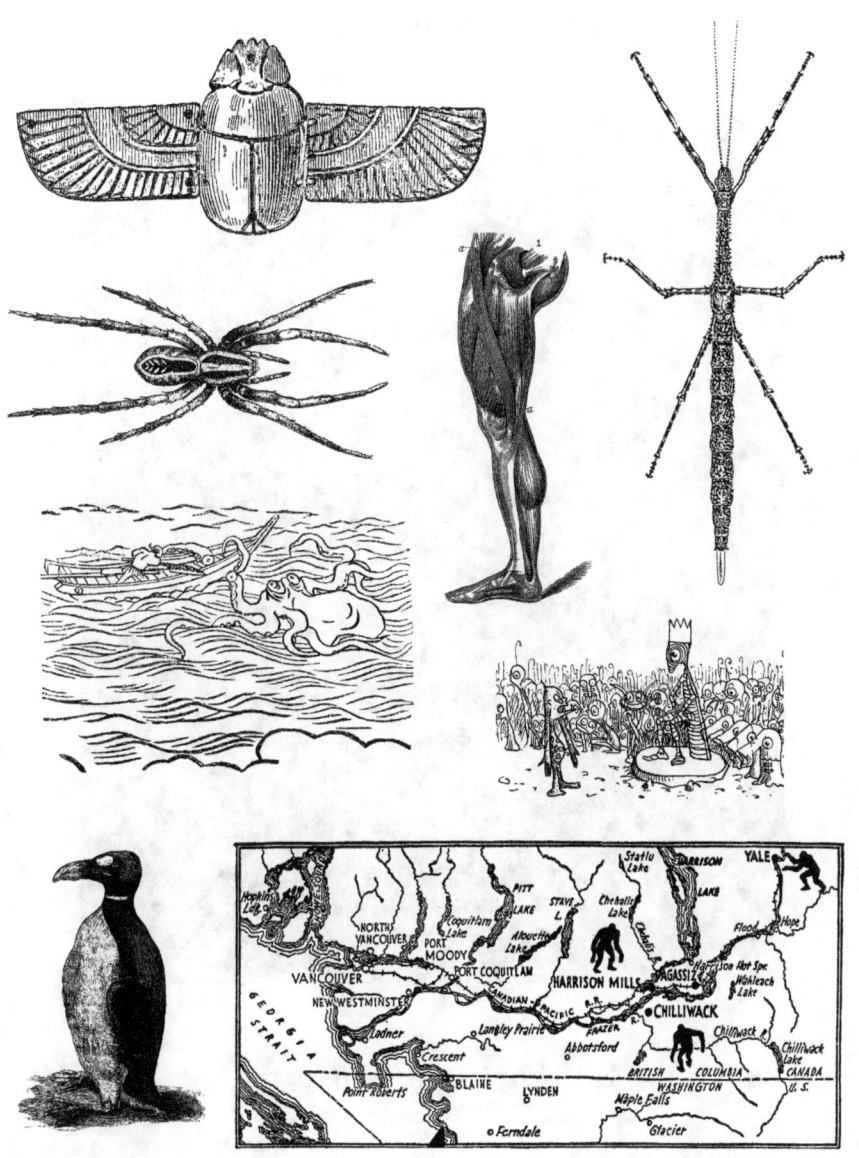

# COACHWHIP PUBLICATIONS

## COACHWHIPBOOKS.COM

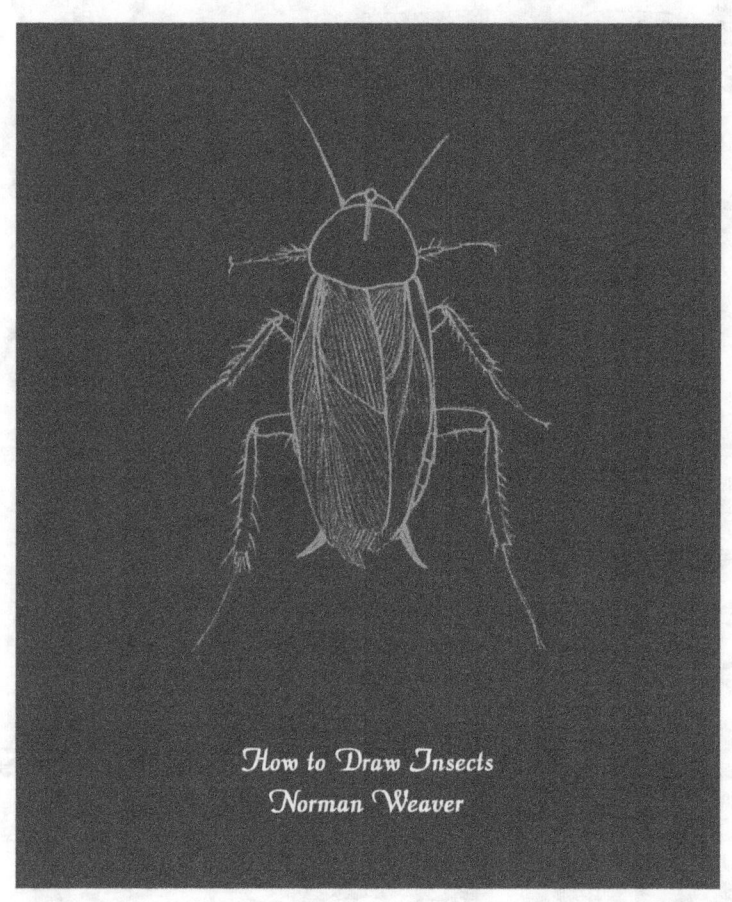

*How to Draw Insects*
*Norman Weaver*

ISBN 978-1-61646-191-1

# COACHWHIP PUBLICATIONS

## COACHWHIPBOOKS.COM

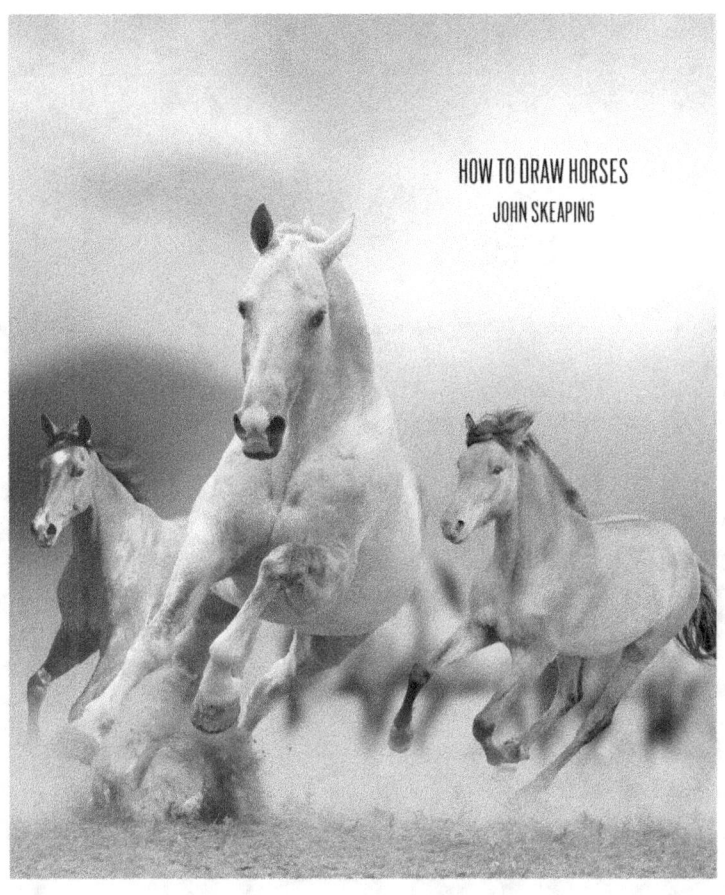

HOW TO DRAW HORSES
JOHN SKEAPING

ISBN 978-1-61646-190-4